AN EMPATH EMPOWERMENT® BOOK

BOOK 1

Empath Empowerment in 30 Days

Rose Rosetree

Women's Intuition Worldwide
Sterling, Virginia

EMPATH EMPOWERMENT IN 30 DAYS

Copyright© 2018 by Rose Rosetree

This book adapts a previously published work by the author, "Become The Most Important Person in the Room: Your 30-Day Plan for Empath Empowerment." The information in this book has been researched over many years. However, the author and publisher assume no liability whatsoever for damages of any kind that occur directly or indirectly from the use of the techniques in this book.

All rights reserved. No part of this book may be reproduced or transmitted in any form or by any means electronic or mechanical, including photocopying and recording, without written permission from the publisher, except for the inclusion of brief passages in a review, forum or blog.

PUBLISHER'S CATALOGING-IN-PUBLICATION

(Publisher's Cataloging-In-Publication Data
(Prepared by The Donohue Group, Inc.)

Names: Rosetree, Rose. | Adaptation of (work): Rosetree, Rose. Become the most important person in the room.
Title: Empath Empowerment in 30 days / Rose Rosetree.
Description: Sterling, Virginia : Women's Intuition Worldwide, [2018] | Series: An Empath Empowerment book ; [1] | "This book adapts a previously published work by the author, 'Become The Most Important Person in the Room: Your 30-Day Plan for Empath Empowerment.'" | Includes index.
Identifiers: ISBN 9781935214465 | ISBN 1935214462 | ISBN 9781935214489 (Kindle) | ISBN 9781935214496 (ebook)
Subjects: LCSH: Sensitivity (Personality trait) | Empathy. | Intuition. | Self-actualization (Psychology) | Aura. | Self-help techniques. | Consciousness.
Classification: LCC BF575.E55 R675 2018 (print) | LCC BF575.E55 (ebook) | DDC 158/.2--dc23

ISBN: 978-1-935214-46-5

LCCN: 2018907782

Please direct all correspondence and inquiries to

Women's Intuition Worldwide, LLC
116 Hillsdale Drive, Sterling, VA 20164-1201
rights@rose-rosetree.com
703-450-9514

VISIT OUR WEBSITE: WWW.ROSE-ROSETREE.COM

Dedication

First there is a mountain.
Then there is no mountain.
Then there is.

So goes a great Buddhist saying. Really, this could be the theme song for any spiritual path that changes lives. Once you decide to experience a closer connection to God, guaranteed, your reality will be shaken, maybe turned inside out. Eventually, that reality will settle back to what it was before, only better.

Now, becoming a skilled empath isn't the same thing as mastering Buddhism or any other religion. Still it counts as a big deal. Do this book right and your reality will be turned inside out, guaranteed. Specifically, you will be turning your reality *right* side out.

I call this Empath Empowerment®. It's a set of skills that you can learn easily, one chapter per day. Our 30-Day Plan for Empath Empowerment is designed to take you through these changes:

- Part One: When you have talent (but little skill) as an empath, *others* are The Most Important Person in The Room.
- Part Two: Developing skill, *you* become The Most Important Person in The Room.
- Part Three: As The Most Important Person in The Room, you can recognize other people with as much clarity as you wish.

How will it feel when you have gained Empath Empowerment? What will change for the better? Come, find out.

Table of Contents

Dedication — iii

PART ONE: Change What Needs Changing — 1

DAY 1.	Get the Picture	3
DAY 2.	Take this Quiz	9
DAY 3.	Be Deep, Sometimes	21
DAY 4.	Delicious Bites	29
DAY 5.	Wakeup Call	33
DAY 6.	The Big Analogy	47

PART TWO: Strengthen Your Way of Being You — 53

DAY 7.	Body Day	55
DAY 8.	Mind Day	61
DAY 9.	Intellect Day	69
DAY 10.	Emotions Day	81
DAY 11.	Spiritual Awareness Day	95
DAY 12.	Soul Day	101
DAY 13.	Bingo	107
DAY 14.	Advanced Bingo	115
DAY 15.	Say Whatever	121
DAY 16.	Turn Life Right Side Out	127
DAY 17.	Better Communication, Your Formula	135
DAY 18.	Gusto	141
DAY 19.	Pass the Test	151

DAY 20.	Hold a Space 157
DAY 21.	Redefine Your Job. 175
DAY 22.	New Eyes. 187

PART THREE: The Fun of Being a Skilled Empath — 199

DAY 23.	Body Language Turned Inside Out. 201
DAY 24.	First-Date Somebody Wonderful 209
DAY 25.	Grounding or Jail 215
DAY 26.	Greed. 225
DAY 27.	Room of Requirement 229
DAY 28.	Magic Picture. 233
DAY 29.	The Master Technique. 247
DAY 30.	Completion 257

Continue Your Discoveries as an Empath — 265

Online Supplement

Meet Our Cast of Characters
Table of Techniques and Quizzes
Table of Illustrations
Index
Advanced Studies for Empaths
More Books by Rose Rosetree

An Unskilled Empath Among Friends

PART ONE

Change What Needs Changing

When you have talent (but little skill) as an empath, *others* can seem like The Most Important Person in The Room.

The nine people folks in our cast of characters? They were all at a party. Someone brought them together for a quick photo. Say that you're the one in the front row, that grayed out person.

Why are "You" looking grayed out? That's what UNSKILLED EMPATHS tend to do without realizing it. Everybody but you seems to be more vivid. To yourself, it's as if you're pictured in lighter shades of gray.

Even if you worry about seeming "selfish" sometimes, you still could be putting yourself last. Part One will help to you find out for sure. Then I'll help you to change what needs changing. Empath Empowerment doesn't happen instantly. But our 30-Day Plan should do it for you… fast as humanly possible…learning quite comfortably… one easy day at a time.

About the 10-minute idea, incidentally. That's an average for your homework. And that 10 minutes of homework is *in addition* to reading this book. Since some of you empaths may read faster than others, and some of you might even choose to reread a particularly choice chapter. Thus, each lesson's *homework* is what I mean by "EE in 30" — 10 minutes a day for 30 days, easing yourself into Empath Empowerment. Sweet!

DAY 1.

Get the Picture

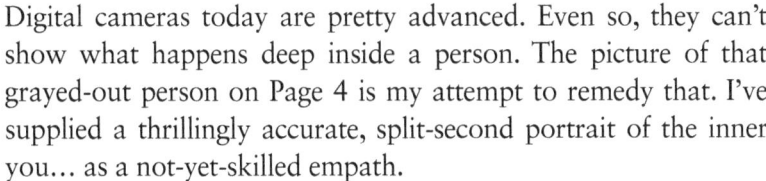

Digital cameras today are pretty advanced. Even so, they can't show what happens deep inside a person. The picture of that grayed-out person on Page 4 is my attempt to remedy that. I've supplied a thrillingly accurate, split-second portrait of the inner you... as a not-yet-skilled empath.

What is happening inside you? I'm asking about your spiritual consciousness, the part of you that's awake inside.

Let's put that question in a more practical way. "When you spend time with others, who gets to be The Most Important Person in The Room?"

Until you become skilled as an empath, the answer probably varies from minute to minute, except for one thing. One person is consistently ignored, underplayed, de-emphasized, under-appreciated: You.

Sure, you'll have an overall sense of self. Outwardly, you may seem just like all the non-empaths in the room, walking and talking and chatting away in Elvish. (Okay, nobody in the room speaks Elvish, empath or not. Although our 30-Day Plan is seriously helpful, I reserve the right to make jokes.)

What is so different about your experience, just because you're an empath? There's an energy awareness of others, a subtext, like watching a TV show where little icons and news-flashes keep popping up at the edges of the screen.

Here are hypothetical examples of those flashy little attention-grabbers. Say that you are visiting with the cast of characters on that earlier page. And all these folks are at a party with you.

Minutes ago, someone has brought you together for the group picture. Afterwards, everybody goes back to partying. What do you notice about them?

ROSCOE, the older guy, dominates the conversation. You feel his energy bouncing off people, large as life and twice as bossy. You notice how others respond to him. Some are starting to feel pretty bad about themselves, the way Roscoe casually disrespects them.

Eventually Roscoe turns his attention to you. On the surface, he appears to be acting polite. Yet intuitively you sense that he doesn't respect you as an equal. As what then? He seems to view you like an unimpressive 10-year-old, none too bright, somebody who mistakenly wandered into this party to watch the grownups.

How you wish that Roscoe would acknowledge you properly. (For one thing, you *are* a grownup now, thank you.) Yet the more you react against Roscoe's image of you, the more you find yourself dumbing down into what he expects. It's like being a chameleon, only scarier.

HANNAH is involved in a friendly, animated conversation. Except, oops, her back sure seems to be hurting like crazy. And she seems anxious, too. Although Hannah hides the discomfort well, somehow you know. If only she felt better!

This wish is made so quickly, you don't consciously remember making it. Consequences follow anyway. (The technical term involves "Taking on someone else's STUFF." We'll discuss that, and how to prevent it, later.)

Meanwhile, **LEXI,** that gorgeous young woman over in the corner, is clearly flirting with James. Wouldn't it be great if you could just enjoy how beautifully she's dressed? Behold that perfect jewelry!\
Even her artless little tee shirt costs about five times as much as

anything you own. Behold and admire... except that will probably be hard. You see, beneath her charming smile, Lexi is also wearing the most annoying, smug air of superiority. What's with that? Exhausting!

As for **JAMES**, he seems pleasant enough. But omigosh, he is lusting after Lexi in the most obvious and embarrassing way. Obvious and embarrassing to you, that is. Outwardly, James may be having a perfectly innocent conversation. He's not even staring, especially. Yet to you, the heat waves are so strong it's amazing that nobody else seems to notice. Even Lexi doesn't quite seem to notice, not at first.

As the sexual charge builds between James and Lexi, there's nothing you can do except, perhaps, try to avoid this tropical corner of the party.

Ever Notice? Sometimes Other People Seem Way Too Intense

When you're an unskilled empath, other people in the room can seem way more vivid than you. Is it common for you to have one or more of the following experiences while you're with others?

- Wondering what it is like to be someone else.
- Experiencing at depth what it feels like to be that person.
- Finding problems, pain or fears, in others. No trying!
- Wishing that things could be better for that other person.
- Wishing that somehow you could help.
- Observing someone's conversation (even if it isn't yours), you automatically notice what's going on beneath the surface.
- When somebody has a negative judgment of you, it may be seem overwhelmingly obvious, no more a secret than if he or she started singing "La Bamba" in a very loud voice.
- You might even slide into *acting* differently, more like the way you're expected to act.

↷ Come to think of it, you may define yourself in that room much as a bat would. Why? You're doing a human version of echolocation. Depending on how you sound to others, that's how you find yourself.

Some Party

And I called this a "party"? Ouch. If you're an unskilled empath, other people in the room with you are in color, while you're more like black-and-white.

Doesn't everybody do that? Not really. NON-EMPATHS naturally put themselves first. They experience *themselves* in vivid color, brighter and more interesting than everyone else.

Granted, a non-empath will occasionally have an insight, such as "I notice things going on beneath the surface of the conversation." While an unskilled empath has insights constantly, and to such an extent that it's like living grayed out — fascinated by everyone else, because even random people appear so much more colorful.

Yet a SKILLED EMPATH gets to be in full color, just like everyone else, and going deeper when we choose. Yes, going deeper as a matter of choice. Otherwise we stay on the surface of life, enjoying the very human privilege of personal vividness in living color.

Before then? Chances are, most of the vividness you experience (verging even on overwhelm, sometimes) really isn't about you at all. Instead you're noticing the inner intensity of other people.

What is the simplest way to understand what it means to be a skilled empath? Maybe this: You learn to make yourself The Most Important Person in The Room. Non-empaths do this from birth. They will always be able do this *more easily* than you. But that doesn't mean they will always do it *better*.

Consider this possibility. Despite not automatically being The Most Important Person in The Room, you possess something else very valuable, something potentially joyful, and even spiritually important. You have at least one important gift as an empath. And that gift is trainable. (Empath gifts will be discussed in more detail tomorrow.)

When you learn how to use your gift(s) on purpose, your quality of life can improve dramatically, compared to what you have now.

The Most Important Person in The Room — you can definitely feel that way (sanely) by becoming a skilled empath.

But getting the full skill set in place takes a 30-Day Plan for Empath Empowerment, not some 10-second summary. For a preview of what to expect, take some Random Snapshots.

Random Snapshots

What does it mean, feeling and acting like The Most Important Person in The Room?

To breathe life into the concept, try the technique I call "Random Snapshots". You can do it whenever two or more people are near you, interacting together.

Observe family, friends, business associates, even strangers — anyone in a room with you and at least two other people. Focus on one of these people at a time. (For this technique, we'll call everyone else but you by the same name, "Pat.")

Observe Pat's body language and expression or just get a vibe. You're not doing hard science here, but noticing in whatever ways come naturally.

Based on what you observe, does Pat feel like The Most Important Person in The Room?

Everyone has the right to feel like The Most Important Person in The Room. Yet not everybody claims that right.

Does Pat seem self-absorbed? That's no insult necessarily. A person can act very politely while being self-absorbed. In fact, a common synonym for that is "self-confident."

Your Assignment for Day 1

Brave Explorer, your assignment is simple. As you deal with people today, take the occasional Random Snapshot with your awareness. Who shows the kind of confidence that suggests feeling like The Most Important Person in The Room?

Within the next 24 hours, will you encounter a single person who can be deeply aware of others (as you naturally are) yet who also shows an easy self-confidence?

Such a person would be a role model for you, a skilled empath.

Skilled empaths are rare… so far. In 30 days, *you* can become one of them. Don't let the scarcity of role models bother you.

DAY 2

Take This Quiz

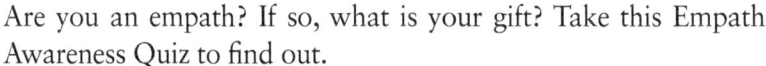

Are you an empath? If so, what is your gift? Take this Empath Awareness Quiz to find out.

Having even one gift would qualify you as a card-carrying empath, with all the rights and privileges to which membership entitles you. Do you have several gifts, just one, or none? By reading the following descriptions, you may relate or not. Answer YES or NO, depending.

I should confess that I have mixed in some descriptions that aren't about being an empath at all. Instead they are popular misunderstandings about being an empath.

Even if you know so much already that you can instantly spot the trick questions, please answer them anyway: If you can relate to each statement that follows, answer YES. Otherwise answer NO.

Empath Awareness Quiz

Can you relate, YES or NO?

1. I can catch another person's mood as easily as if I'm catching a yawn.
2. Although I don't feel other people's feelings, I sure know what those feelings are. For instance, I might know that the other person is lying, or clueless, or feeling five different things all at once.

3. Much of the time, I feel lost and alone, sometimes even miserable.
4. I can always tell if a woman is promiscuous, even if she's nicely dressed.
5. When I hike in a forest and the trees or animals are suffering, I can feel it.
6. I might actually be part chameleon, because I talk differently with different people, using bigger words or smaller. I'll give different examples, depending. Like when I'm with an artist, colors seem brighter. With a musician, I notice sounds more than usual.
7. Back at catching things, I have been known to catch other people's headaches or other physical symptoms. I guess I'm suggestible. Could I even be a hypochondriac?
8. I don't necessarily catch other people's aches and pains but I can be with someone and start feeling pressure or pain in different parts of my body.
9. I might have a selfish version of this. Nothing happens in my own body but I'll be pretty sure, sometimes, that another person is tired or hurts somewhere physically.
10. Sometimes I can tell things about people spiritually without having to ask, e.g., A person has something to prove spiritually, or hates the subject of religion, or has a strong spiritual connection.
11. I love fantasy novels, so naturally I'm intrigued when I see people describing themselves as a Fallen Angel Empath or an Artist Empath (where "Everything you touch turns to song and is freed by the color of your eyes.") When I find examples like these on the Internet, I could read for hours. I wonder if I could be all these different types of empath.
12. I'll be with a friend and suddenly I'll be like, "Life is good." or "Life is bad." Feelings like these can just flicker through me, depending on whoever I'm with. Another weird one is that, out of nowhere, I might have the feeling "God loves me." Or "God is scary." This happens

all on its own. Nobody around me is having some "big, serious conversation about what I believe." I just have these random experiences in the back of my mind. Could that happen because I am some kind of empath?

13. Talk about discomfort, un-watered plants drive me crazy. I can practically hear them scream.
14. It bothers me when people mistreat machines, like computers or cars. Some people think nothing of forcing machines, kicking them, calling them names. This upsets me, even if I don't own the machine and won't have to pay for fixing it later.
15. Caring is the sign of an empath, isn't it? When I always root for the underdog and cry when I watch movies, what kind of empath does that make me?
16. I'm really good at Emotional Intelligence. I can label anger, sadness, rage, happiness, etc., whether it belongs to me or not. Which empath ability makes me so good at this?
17. Dysfunctional patterns learned during childhood have caused me to anticipate what other people need.
18. Holding a crystal is magical for me; the same thing with precious gemstones. They take me on an energy ride, showing me different ways to be.
19. Body language tells me everything I need to know. Anyone talented like me finds it very easy to figure out from expression if somebody likes you, is a bad person, etc. In five seconds, I can learn everything that matters.
20. I'm just glad people wear different clothes from each other. Otherwise, I'd have a really hard time telling them apart.

Quiz Answers

1. I can catch another person's mood as easily as if I'm catching a yawn.

YES, Emotional Oneness is my name for that gift. I'm delighted to learn that you are a fellow sufferer. Kidding about the suffering part. This is a wonderful empath gift, no weirder than any of the others. With all empath gifts, once you get skills you can help other people elegantly. (And without suffering.)

2. Although I don't feel other people's feelings, I sure know what those feelings are. For instance, I might know that the other person is lying, or clueless, or feeling five different things all at once.

YES, you have Emotional Intuition, a gift for appreciating people's emotions at a distance. Ever wonder how people can get away with lying to others about emotions? Not everyone — not even every empath — has Emotional Intuition or Emotional Oneness.

3. Much of the time, I feel lost and alone, sometimes even miserable.

NO. Being an empath need not involve misery. Even being an *unskilled empath* doesn't necessarily involve misery; it's just that your life can improve a lot once you become skilled. Maybe this book will take you from *pretty happy* to *outrageously happy.*

By contrast, you could be miserable for reasons that have nothing at all to do with being an empath, like puberty or having a bad hair day.

4. I can always tell if a woman is promiscuous, even if she's nicely dressed.

NO, sorry, this isn't necessarily about being an empath, either. It could be a matter of psychological projection. If you specialize in noticing a particular kind of problem in others, you may have some unfinished business.

And if you are "always" running into people with a particular kind of sexual problem or anger management issues, control issues, narcissism, etc., I would definitely encourage you to seek help from a mental health professional.

5. *When I hike in a forest and the trees or animals are suffering, I can feel it.*

YES, you are an Environmental Empath if you notice the beauty or suffering — or just plain specialness — of a forest.

As this type of empath, you'll feel quite different at the beach, in the desert, or pounding pavement in a big city. I don't mean having varied experiences depending on whether you're a news reporter or mortician but, rather, an inner quality that shifts.

Your thinking could be subtly different, or different environments could alter how you feel in your body, how you walk, or what you hear in the silence around you.

Also, YES, you are Animal Empath if sometimes you connect to the inner world of animals. This could happen with all God's creatures or just one particular kind of animal, like ferrets.

Animal Empaths know that each animal or pet has a distinctive way to be. With this gift, you appreciate the animal's experience on a deep level, like knowing when your favorite ferret is excited, frightened, or joyful. As an empath, you're not just observing behavior from the outside but connecting intuitively to something deeper.

6. *I might actually be part chameleon, because I talk differently with different people, using bigger words or smaller. I'll give different examples, depending. Like when I'm with an artist, colors seem brighter. With a musician, I notice sounds more than usual.*

YES, you have described the gift (and challenge) of being an Intellectual Empath. Intuitively you understand how different people think — not reading specific thoughts in their minds but sensing how to reach that person best. Until skilled, you may feel like a chameleon but, trust me, you are no reptile.

7. Back at catching things, I have been known to catch other people's headaches or other physical symptoms. I guess I'm suggestible. Could I even be a hypochondriac?

YES, you are a Messy, Suggestible, Hypochondriacal Empath. Wait, that's not my official name for this gift. Not at all. Instead I call it Physical Oneness. Once you are skilled, it's a very valuable gift, being able to experience other people's problems in your own body — just during the short duration of a Skilled Empath Merge. Wait and see.

8. I don't necessarily feel other people's aches and pains but I can be with someone and start feeling pressure or pain in different parts of my body.

YES, this also counts as an empath gift. It is the gift I just called Physical Oneness. Some empaths receive information about others in the form of direct physical sensations, but not always. This isn't necessarily a one-on-one equation, like "her stomachache = my stomachache." It could be more like "her worrying = my stomachache."

As a skilled empath, you'll learn to interpret these symbolic physical experiences, finding out what the true message is.

You'll also learn how to avoid personally taking on "information" just because you happen to be near somebody who feels bad. What a relief, turning your gifts OFF or ON purposely! After all, how busy do you want your body to be? Wouldn't it be nice to just feel normal (whatever that is for you)?

9. I have a selfish version of this. Nothing happens in my own body but I'll be pretty sure, sometimes, that another person is tired or hurts somewhere physically.

YES, only don't call this gift "Selfish Empathy" because you can help people with it, just like any other empath gift. Instead, might I recommend? Call this gift Physical Intuition.

The name means that you know what is happening to other people's bodies. You happen to receive this information at a distance, rather than downloading the data directly through sensations in your own personal body.

10. Sometimes I can tell things about people spiritually without having to ask, e.g., A person has something to prove spiritually, or hates the subject of religion, or has a strong spiritual connection.

YES, count this as Spiritual Intuition. The jumping-off-point could be as simple as looking at the person's forehead or hearing his/her voice. Of course, this knowledge about religion would be something other than empath talent if the person happens to be wearing a very large cross or a turban.

11. I love fantasy novels, so naturally I'm intrigued when I see people describing themselves as a Fallen Angel Empath or an Artist Empath (where "Everything you touch turns to song and is freed by the color of your eyes.") When I find words like these on the Internet, I could read for hours. I wonder if I could be all these different types of empath.

NO, because having an interest in colorful names like these involves fantasy fiction more than being an honest-to-goodness empath with real-life experiences.

It's not about being an empath if you are fascinated by horses or spaceships or brown paper packages tied up with string. Nothing about your lifestyle reveals whether or not you are an empath.

12. I'll be with someone and suddenly I'll be like, "Life is good." or "Life is bad." Feelings like this can just flicker through me, depending on whom I'm with. Another weird one is that, out of nowhere, I might have the feeling "God loves me." or "God is scary." This happens all on its own. Nobody around me is having some "big, serious conversation about what I believe." I just have these random experiences in the back of my mind. Could that happen because I am some kind of empath?

YES. Good catch! This is Spiritual Oneness. In the past you may not always have connected these subtle inner experiences to the people they came from. A skilled empath would. In fact, as a skilled empath, you can also stop having random experiences like these. Unskilled Spiritual Oneness can cause a deep kind of worry that is hard to shake until you get skills.

13. Talk about discomfort, un-watered plants drive me crazy. I can practically hear them scream.

YES, you're a Plant Empath. This gift could help you to garden. Or to cook.

14. It bothers me when people mistreat machines, like computers or cars. People think nothing of forcing the machines, kicking them, calling them names. This upsets me, even if I don't own the machine and won't have to pay for fixing it later.

YES, count this as being a Mechanical Empath (when you care about the machine, not when you do the kicking). Every machine contains its own consciousness, and it may even have its own deva, an elemental intelligence assigned to it.

As a Mechanical Empath, you can move into the consciousness of that machine. Intuitively you know what will fix it. With skill, the problems of machines will stop feeling like your personal problems.

15. Caring is the sign of an empath, isn't it? When I always root for the underdog and cry when I watch movies, what kind of empath does that make me?

NO, caring and crying can happen for many reasons. An empath moves in and out of the direct experience of what it is like to be someone else. This can be quite subtle, and need not involve drama of any kind.

16. I'm really good at Emotional Intelligence. I can label anger, sadness, rage, happiness, etc., whether it belongs to me or not. Which empath ability makes me so good at this?

Congratulations but NO, being good at Emotional Intelligence doesn't bear any relationship to being an empath. Anyone can learn the skill set of Emotional Intelligence, but that won't solve an empath's biggest problem, which is the need to remove pain belonging to others from your aura.

17. Dysfunctional patterns learned during childhood have caused me to anticipate what other people need.

NO, this has nothing to do with being an empath, either. Here's the only connection: If you were born as an empath, you learned to anticipate at greater depth than a non-empath.

Let's clear up a popular misunderstanding. Empath abilities are not dysfunctional patterns, nor are they learned.

Instead, being an empath shows in your aura right from the time you're in the womb. I'm not joking. You can check this out for yourself, since everyone (empath or not) can learn to read auras.

With that skill set, try reading auras of pregnant women, in person or from photos, separating out the information belonging to mother and child, or mother and twins. Every human being has a very distinctive energy field, and it's filled with information. Some of this changes, some doesn't.

I can teach you to read auras, whatever the horrors or joys of your childhood. I can teach you to develop Emotional Intelligence. But I cannot make you into an empath.

18. Holding a crystal is magical for me; the same thing with precious gemstones. They take me on an energy ride, showing me different ways to be.

YES, you're a Crystal Empath. Gemstones carry fascinating energy properties. With this gift, you'll experience a shift in consciousness just by picking up the stone, closing your eyes, and paying attention to what happens next.

Incidentally, this form of intuitive travel has nothing to do with whether you like reading books about the energy properties of different crystals.

19. Body language tells me everything I need to know. Anyone talented like me finds it very easy to figure out from expression if somebody likes you, is a bad person, etc. In five seconds, I can learn everything that matters.

NO, sorry, this is not the gift of an empath. Certainty that you instantly know everything about another person is actually the opposite. Empaths tend to be explorers, not stereotypers.

One way to see what I mean by this is to peek ahead at Day 23 and "Body Language Turned Inside Out." You'll enjoy this chapter whether you are an empath or not.

20. I'm just glad people wear different clothes from each other. Otherwise, I'd have a really hard time telling them apart.

NO, you're probably not an empath of any kind. But you might have a bright future as a fashion designer.

Congratulations

You've completed the most complicated part of this entire book. More important, what have you learned about yourself? Even one gift as an empath qualifies you as a card-carrying empath.

So, what else do you need to know right away?

That card is invisible.

You have the right to remain silent. Anything you say can and will be used against you — wait, those are Miranda Rights that a police officer will read before carrying you away.

Empath Rights are just the same as anyone else's, including free will, the pursuit of God and happiness, seeking a good life the best way you know.

For you, becoming a Skilled Empath might just turn out to be one of those ways.

Your Assignment for Day 2

Brave Explorer, think about your gift(s) as an empath. Do you notice anyone else who seems to have the same gift(s) as you? What about friends of yours who might have different empath gifts?

Educate them, if you wish. Probably they have never discussed what it means to be an empath. Or they think that "empath" always means "taking on other people's emotions." Yet one more misunderstanding that is common among beginners!

Most empath gifts aren't about emotions at all. Play around with all these cool new names:

- Animal Empath
- Crystal Empath
- Emotional Intuition
- Emotional Oneness
- Environmental Empath
- Intellectual Empath
- Mechanical Empath
- Physical Intuition
- Physical Oneness
- Plant Empath
- Spiritual Intuition
- Spiritual Oneness

These names will come in handy, starting with what we explore tomorrow. Remember, if you have even one of these gifts, that qualifies you to consider yourself an empath. Whatever the gift…

An empath has a gift
for directly experiencing
what it is like to be someone else.

That's what it means. That simple. That fascinating.

DAY 3

Be Deep, Sometimes

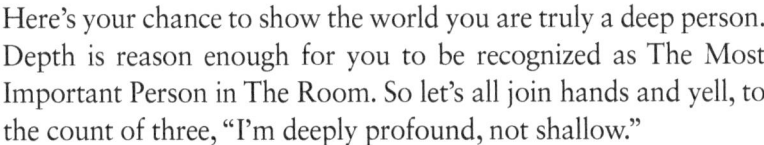

Here's your chance to show the world you are truly a deep person. Depth is reason enough for you to be recognized as The Most Important Person in The Room. So let's all join hands and yell, to the count of three, "I'm deeply profound, not shallow."

Wait, that won't work, will it? Consider:

1. Deep people don't need to do things like cheerleading in order to prove they are deep. To be "deep" means that you go within, rather than taking your cues from others. Really, for human life, the opposite of "deep" isn't shallow. It's "wide," as in social and friendly and connected to the world outside of your inner self.
2. You don't become The Most Important Person in The Room by asking anyone else for permission, recognition, etc.
3. Deep people don't just do things like follow someone else's command to act like best buddies. First you want to know why. And then you make your own choice.

So let's clear up this social thing once and for all. To become skilled as an empath, you don't need to show the world anything. Empath Empowerment isn't about personal image, like whether or not you dress with attitude. Being skilled as an empath doesn't hinge on social choices of any kind.

How do I know? Surveys, for one thing. Wherever in the world I teach Empath Empowerment, I'll conduct the following survey. Let's try it now.

Boundary Survey

Raise your hand if:

1. You have tried to tighten up your boundaries with other people.
2. You have tried to stop being overly sensitive.
3. You have attempted to visualize a mirror or façade or bubble — any kind of invisible shield.
4. You have tried to protect yourself by avoiding people who drain energy, like narcissists and psychic vampires.

This far into the Survey, I find that most people's hands go up. Has yours? To continue:

5. Now, raise your other hand if this has helped you much.

Interpreting the Results

Usually, very few hands go up.

Of course, everyone *wants* to raise hands. Hardworking empaths don't want to feel as though they have failed. It's especially humiliating not to raise your hand because "everyone knows" that socially-based approaches, like "boundaries," represent your only hope for a balanced life.

Wrong. They are not your only hope. Actually, for reasons you'll soon understand, those boundary-based approaches aren't much use at all, not for empaths.

Boundary-type approaches don't work very well. Not for empaths, anyway.

Brave Explorer, I'm going to teach you how to *use the power of your consciousness* to become a skilled empath.

In my experience, this is the only approach that really works. What do the contrasting approaches in our Boundary Survey have in common? They're social.

That means wide, not deep.

What does it mean to be an empath, anyway? Unlike non-empaths, since birth you have journeyed in consciousness, tripping in and out of other people's auras.

Is this done consciously? Not when you're *unskilled*. Which is why I call this kind of journeying UNSKILLED EMPATH MERGE.

The travel isn't done slowly and deliberately, like planning a trip to Disney World. Nonetheless, as an empath you're wired to make super-quick, super-deep journeys in consciousness. Unskilled Empath Merges happen spontaneously, and at random, from birth.

The learning part is lovely, and you may also be helping people with every journey (although at a high personal cost). But there's one problem, for sure. With every unskilled empath merge, you'll pick up STUFF from the other person. It will move from that other person's aura into your own.

Unskilled empath merges happen at a different frequency from social behavior. Being with other people, working hard to firm up your boundaries, what's to keep your aura from spreading out into an unskilled empath merge? Nothing.

Socially-based approaches aren't bad, but they work much better for **non-empaths**, the ones who don't pop in and out of other people's auras by means of consciousness. Ironic, isn't it?

Today's project is to start claiming the power of your consciousness. This power was always available, if only you knew how to use it.

Be Deep

Here is an exercise to activate the power of your consciousness. (Please, if you are just browsing and don't plan to actually do the exercise yet, skip immediately to the next chapter. This exercise is for doing, not skimming.)

Read through the following points. Then do them, taking the occasional peek as needed.

Oh yes, first close the door. Do whatever it takes to be alone without anyone else clamoring for your attention. Turn off the background music, your computer and all those other electronic companions. Elvis will have to leave the building.

1. Sit comfortably. Uncross your legs or arms or any other place you are pretzeling. Put out your cigarette. Park your gum. You're gonna go deep, and go it alone. Woo-hoo!
2. Close your eyes for about 10 seconds.
3. Open your eyes.
4. Close your eyes for about 20 seconds.
5. Open your eyes.
6. Close your eyes for about 30 seconds.
7. Open your eyes.

You're done for now, so let's compare notes.

Deep? Whatever

Think about what just happened while your eyes were closed. This wasn't a wildly dramatic experience, was it? What matters is that, whatever happened, you were experiencing it with your *consciousness* — the part of you that keeps awake deep inside.

With eyes closed, you could have noticed thoughts, sounds, emotions, physical sensations. You could have heard words in your head, seen colors or images. You could have felt space or heard silence, heard space or felt silence.

To use a technical term, we can call any of these experiences *"whatever."* Any whatever would be fine. You could even have had more than one whatever at a time.

Consciousness lies beneath every whatever, just as this page you're reading contains words printed on it and blank space beneath. We need that blank space in order to see the words. Similarly, we need consciousness inside to be able to notice every passing thought, sound, emotion, etc.

Did you notice how easily you could have your eyes closed and notice things? Effort isn't necessary for an experience to count. Neither is drama.

It isn't as though *nothing* happens with your eyes closed unless you see a tall, skinny guy with purple hair and black clothes, a clueless sort of person who rides his skateboard really fast and then crashes into you. *Consciousness is subtle.*

Back at our previous exercise, trying hard is the only way you could have messed it up. If that happened, your "punishment" is to do the exercise again, only relax this time.

Repeat "Be Deep" if:

- You were struggling for inner drama like a close encounter with the crashing skateboard guy
- Or you blamed yourself for having thoughts
- Or you gave yourself a headache due to trying so hard
- Or you tried sneaking in other techniques you have learned because you couldn't stand going for three seconds naked in consciousness without dressing yourself up in something extra-fancy.

Go back, Brave Explorer. Dare to be simple and do our Be Deep exercise once more. And when you have managed to do the simple, sloppy, effortless technique, such as it is....

Hello

Imagine a fairy tale where the Great Flying Turkey (or some other being of enormous spiritual power and compassion) has just touched you with his magic wand, awakening you from The Enchantment.

Ta da!

Using Be Deep, you have done the magic act on your own. You have reminded your conscious mind that your consciousness is *you*. I mean a deep down version of you, independent of any social situation.

This version of you isn't obvious but subtle. You may not feel absolutely convinced that you have had "an experience" in the way you would if, for instance, you had just been run over by a truck.

That's a good thing, and I don't only mean the lack of tire tracks all over your body. For anything that I teach you, don't be sure. Be sloppy. Now you officially have permission.

If you already meditate, or pray powerfully, or read auras, you are familiar with using your consciousness on purpose in order to accomplish something. Becoming a skilled empath will also involve using your consciousness, but differently.

Your Assignment for Day 3

Today's assignment is to become more comfortable with your consciousness.

It's simple. It's deep. It requires no effort for you to notice it, merely a subtle shift of attention.

Once you're familiar with consciousness, shifting to an inner awareness is no harder than picking up a phone and saying, "Hello."

Brave Explorer, once you're familiar with consciousness, you can aim it in any direction you like. And, in future chapters, you'll be doing a lot more of that.

Does aiming your consciousness mean forcing or pushing? No way. It's simply being.

Let's review what makes non-doing, this simple thing, so important:

- Turning your empath gifts OFF or ON effectively requires that you actively use your consciousness.
- Avoiding toxic people isn't about consciousness. It's a social skill.
- Firming up your boundaries with others, like refusing to buy candy bars for your neighbor or become her love slave — that isn't about consciousness either.
- Only consciousness can keep you clear inside yourself and make you The Most Important Person in The Room.

With today's assignment, you'll do the Be Deep exercise at random intervals during the day until you feel comfortable with it. Either do the version we've covered so far or you use the version on the next page. That Be Deep Quickie will take even less time.

As a skilled empath, mostly you won't be paying attention to your consciousness. Occasionally you will make a subtle shift or two, then let go.

That occasional, effortless, expert tweak to your consciousness is the essence of Empath Empowerment. And Be Deep Quickie can help you to become familiar with this gigantic, free, inner resource.

Be Deep Quickie

This is a super-fast way to become conscious of your consciousness.
1. Close your eyes for about 1 second.
2. Open your eyes.
3. Close your eyes for about 2 seconds.
4. Open your eyes.
5. Close your eyes for about 3 seconds.
6. Open your eyes.

Notice this: One thing has been the same whether your eyes were open or closed. You. Your inner consciousness has been there. It always will be there. That's the point!

Also notice: When your eyes are closed, consciousness is directed within. Many experiences are possible, such as thoughts, feelings, physical sensations. These "whatevers" happen effortlessly.

You can always choose to be conscious of your consciousness. You can notice whatevers as part of it. You can pay attention to consciousness now and forget about it later. No damage will result. Consciousness will be available for your notice whenever you choose to notice.

Grab a Be Deep Quickie whenever you wish. Every time, always, for life... you have that wonderful inner resource called "consciousness."

Take five or more random breaks today to Be Deep, slow version or quick, as you wish. Tomorrow, we'll take your experience further.

DAY 4

Delicious Bites

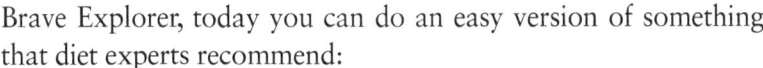

Brave Explorer, today you can do an easy version of something that diet experts recommend:

"Order that super-rich dessert. Take your first bite and stop to savor the taste. First bites are always the most delicious part of any dessert. If you do it right, really tasting, one bite or two is all you need. Then you'll be perfectly satisfied."

Just a bite or two, right? Such a heroic idea! Unfortunately, if you're like me, in real life you'll settle for many additional bites, even if they don't taste quite so good as that first fork of fudge cake. Some of us (and I do mean me, here) just might stuff ourselves silly. Possibly we'll pack in those inferior bites until an entire cake is gone.

Certain life experiences are so gosh-darned delicious that it can be really hard to say "Stop. I enjoyed this, but enough is enough."

Shopping can be one of those experiences. So can video games. Admit it, you too have certain favorite can't-stop activities in life. But did you ever think that empathic hitch-hiking might be one of them?

Empathic Hitch-Hiking

It happens whenever an empath moves into the experience of being another person, pet, plant, etc. If you find cake hard to avoid, that's nothing compared to the strange escapist pleasure of spontaneous unskilled empath merge.

It happens so fast, the term "split second" is too slow. Divide one split second into a thousand "shards." One shard, that's how fast it happens.

During this shard of time, an unskilled empath spontaneously merges auras with someone — anyone — in the room. So long as you're an unskilled empath, this super-fast empathic hitch-hiking occurs whenever you're with people.

The good news is, you gain a deep knowledge of what it is like to be those people. The bad news? Knowledge is stored subconsciously, where it will do your conscious mind no good at all.

Worse, unskilled empath merge causes your aura to takes on some fear or pain that originally belonged to the other person. You bring back this STUFF (subconsciously, of course) as a kind of souvenir. There it stays indefinitely, stuck in your aura. **IMPORTED STUFF!**

Remember our idea from Day 3? Empaths need to use consciousness to become skilled. So it isn't enough to adjust your social behavior. If you try hard to firm up your boundaries, you'll only manage to make nice firm boundaries around the STUFF that enters regardless.

A very skilled aura reader can tell the difference. Let's use the example of Hannah's aura. She has worked so hard at her boundaries that she has formed one wall around her Heart Chakra and two walls around her Solar Plexus Chakra.

The location and number of walls in an aura will depend on the ways that a person has worked to make her artificial boundaries.

Wherever they're located, Hannah's walls *do* make it hard for her friends to get close to her.

Meanwhile, those walls *don't* prevent Hannah from empathic hitch-hiking and picking up Imported STUFF.

Ironic, isn't it?

Phew! Instead of that all-too-popular approach, let's explore Empath Empowerment®, with skills *based in consciousness*, rather than changing outer behavior or creating visualizations that further clutter up an aura.

I'm going to help you to take more of an interest in yourself. As a result, you will gradually stop aura-level hitch-hiking, finding it more rewarding to drive your own car.

Can we stop here? Is it enough to intellectually understand the concept?

Sorry, no. You'll need to learn specific skills for using consciousness actively, paying prime quality attention to yourself. Let's start to build on what you did yesterday with Be Deep and the Be Deep Quickie.

Quality Time with Yourself

This simple technique can help you develop skill at directing your consciousness in a natural, effortless way. For just a few seconds:

1. Stop whatever you're doing.
2. Close your eyes.
3. And pay attention to whatever you happen to notice about yourself.

That's it, nothing fancy at all.

Notice?

Quality Time With Yourself does not involve saying words like, "I'm being aware of myself." Nor is this self-hypnosis. Instead you're tasting your own presence.

How will that taste?

- You might encounter energy. Or silence.
- Or emotions. Or physical sensations.
- Or more than one thing. Maybe many things, all of them about you.
- If you happen to have a thought about someone or something other than yourself, that's okay. Just be more interested in whatever you notice about *you*.
- You might feel as if you are slowing time down just a bit.
- It could feel like "me time," because you are interested in something (anything) about yourself.

This moment of Quality Time With Yourself is mainly about being, not changing how you think, nor improving yourself, and actually not doing anything in particular.

Don't worry about having some big, flashy mystical experience. Paying attention to yourself, with consciousness, is really quite ordinary. If you have thoughts, that's okay. (Note: You're also allowed to have skin.)

Your Assignment for Day 4

Quality time isn't quantity time. So today's assignment won't take long.

To succeed at this exercise, all you will need is one minute's time to be aware of yourself. So how about doing that three different times today?

Quality Time With Yourself could be compared to having a few bites of delicious cake. Get the flavor of *you*, right now, right in the moment. Of course, you'll be tasting consciousness, not a crave-making, sweet-tooth-tickling dessert.

To become a skilled empath, you don't have to spend every waking moment gloating over your own consciousness. An occasional taste can be plenty, like that first bite of cake.

DAY 5

Wakeup Call

"Operator, give me a wakeup call at 7:00 a.m."

Isn't that a delightful perk of staying in a hotel? I love being able to ask for that special help with getting up in the morning. Today, I'm going to teach you a way to wake up your inner self, effortlessly moving out STUFF that never really belonged to you, Imported STUFF that sneaked in because you were a talented empath but not yet skilled.

First though, let's delve more thoroughly into how STUFF sneaks into an unskilled empath's aura. To illustrate my explanation, here come pictures of two people — "You" and Lexi — with auras included. *Turn the page* and you'll see them.

Note: I have smooshed both bodies and auras so they can fit into the space available. This is a symbolic illustration made for teaching purposes. No body parts or aura chunks have really been amputated.

At first glance, the auras belonging to Lexi and "You" might look identical. Except "You," on the left, are an empath. The dotted line at the edge of your aura is meant to symbolize your ultra-refined, quick moving energy field.

Compared to a non-empath, your entire aura has a relatively refined, porous texture, moving at a faster rate of vibration. All empaths have that kind of aura. Lexi is the gal on the right, a non-empath, a.k.a. "normal person." Her aura is just as good, only not refined in this particular way, so no dotted line for her, just a regular line. See that?

The High-Vibe Aura Of an Empath

Basics about Auras and "STUFF"

Just because you're doing our 30-Day Plan doesn't mean you know all about aura reading. So here are some basics you'll need to know as an empath.

Everyone's aura contains major chakras, centers of information that correspond to certain parts of your body, like Throat Chakra or Heart Chakra. One of my favorite discoveries after decades of teaching how to read auras is that each major chakra contains 50 different databanks of information; minor chakras have 50 chakra databanks, too.

To picture all those databanks, think of a pipe organ, where every one of the 50 pipes can be a different size, play a different note.

Each chakra databank contains two types of information. There will be a GIFT of your soul, something you can do beautifully. GIFTS in auras are permanent, no work involved, like having fingerprints. Incidentally, those GIFTS include your empath gift(s).

Unfortunately, each aura databank can also show problems. This second type of information includes problems related to dozens of kinds of STUFF for which RES Energy HEALING Skills provide solutions, such as:

- Negative Thought Forms left over from childhood.
- Frozen Blocks of Stuck Energy, brought to you by your ex, or your boss, or any tough relationship.
- Cords of Attachment, e.g., Energy tubes between your aura and the auras of all your significant others, structures that replay old patterns of pain 24/7 — like a nightmare sound file run amok.

You get the idea. I had to find a technical term for all these short- and long-term patterns that can clog up an aura. So I have chosen the term STUFF. At any given time, a person's aura will contain a combination of GIFTS of your soul and STUFF.

STUFF can always be healed. But that requires expert help. Until it is healed, STUFF makes life much less fun.

In our diagram on the facing page, the squiggles represent stored-up STUFF in both people's auras. Check it out.

When you, a born empath, hang out with another person like Lexi, a kind of reflex action happens between your aura and hers. Your aura surrounds it, giving a kind of hug. As described yesterday, the technical term for this is an unskilled empath merge. You'll see a sample of this illustrated *when you turn the page*.

Remember how long that takes? Just one shard of time. So an unskilled empath merge isn't even conscious.

Nurturing, supporting, extending friendship or love, seeking understanding... ah, it's a beautiful thing. Except more than that happens, as you may guess after taking a peek at our second illustration *after you turn the page*.

Automatically, after doing an unskilled empath merge, you will take some of that other person's STUFF back into your aura. Turn the page and you'll see what I mean.

Yikes!

See what I mean about empathic hitch-hiking?

If you look carefully, you'll see what happens after unskilled empath merge. Now Lexi's aura contains less STUFF. Nice for her!

Sadly, many squiggles of her STUFF (not all of them, but plenty) have gone into "Your" aura.

In this series of illustrations, squiggles are drawn differently on "You" and Lexi just to clarify that concept. In reality, STUFF is blobby, some bits bigger and some bits smaller, and none quite so artistic looking as what has been shown here.

STUFF in Auras

DURING
An Unskilled Empath Merge

AFTER
An Unskilled Empath Merge

Empath
(You)

Non-Empath
(Lexi)

Attractively drawn or not, STUFF isn't lovely to wear inside your energy field. Frankly, the very idea of suck-in with other people's STUFF (whether nicely drawn or not) is…

Just a Bit Disgusting

And it may not cheer you up to realize that all this has been happening throughout your entire life. Probably it has happened without your consciously noticing the aura dynamics, either. How come?

- The process itself isn't conscious. Instead, it's on the level of auras and subconscious awareness.
- No effort is required. Unskilled empath merges happen totally automatically.
- And they happen really fast, in just one quick shard of time.

Exactly How Long Has This Been Happening?

Merely every day of your life.

Merely repeatedly, within each day.

Yep, that's how things have been for you. Now's a good time to learn about this, however, since you're doing this 30-Day Plan. Otherwise it might be just a bit depressing, learning the aura-level truth: Long as you've been wired as an empath… and as long as you possessed merely talent, not skill… you couldn't keep this STUFF-slurping reflex from occurring. Quite automatically.

Okay, maybe sometimes you noticed what was happening, in a vague way. Looking back, maybe it seemed to you that Lexi was special; during your visit she seemed more vivid to you than, well, you.

Or, maybe later, after that visit, somehow you might have felt drained.

What if a YouTube video had somehow captured the behavior of your aura during this visit? Here's what viewers would see happening during your unskilled empath merge with Lexi. During that shard of time:

1. Your empath gift(s) randomly switch ON.
2. Causing your aura to expand until it surrounds Lexi's aura.
3. Your aura pulls some of her STUFF right out of her aura, depositing those icky things directly into your own, personal, energy field.
4. Next, the edges of your aura return to normal, surrounding your body only.
5. Only you keep a little souvenir every time, some bits of STUFF formerly belonging to Lexi. Oops!

Well, So What?

On learning about this, your first reaction might be, "How sweet! Unskilled empath merges represent my beautiful, spontaneous service to humanity. Doing these STUFF pickups could be considered the ultimate in selfless, heroic, incognito volunteer work."

Except how much does it really help the other person?

Consider Lexi, for instance. Within a couple of hours, at most, she'll quickly replace the subconscious fear, anger, pain etc. that you lifted from her.

Why? Since Lexi hasn't consciously chosen to heal or learn anything. Therefore, no depth healing was possible.

Meanwhile you, the empath, may have done a good deed, very temporarily. Unfortunately, you'll pay a price.

Every time.

You see, the long-term effect is to clog up your aura with somebody else's STUFF.

(To see what I mean, *flip back to that last diagram* and take another look. Isn't that something! Erggg.)

Every bit of that STUFF from unskilled empath merge causes suffering for you.

How Is that Fair?

Hey, don't even ask. That is one useless question, on a par with asking, "But why does gravity have to point down? Boo-hoo."

In our next chapter, I'll explain why I think all this happens. In no chapter of this book, however, will I promise that life is fair. Not short-term, anyway.

But in this chapter I'm about to teach you the simplest thing you can do about the problem that we could call "When porous box contains other people's squiggles." (Also known as "Imported STUFF.")

You see, what I've shown you with these diagrams is how an unskilled empath does those super-quick, not-conscious, unskilled empath merges. Which result in randomly picking up other people's STUFF.

By contrast, a skilled empath avoids picking up Imported STUFF. So most of our 30-Day Plan will emphasize changing that habit of turning empath gifts ON, which results in unskilled empath merges and Imported STUFF.

Today's skill, however, is a useful workaround. After you have pulled Imported STUFF into your aura from an unintentional, unskilled empath merge, you can use the Wakeup Call technique to rid you of that nasty STUFF.

Why Call It "Wakeup Call"?

Because, Brave Explorer, this technique works like a wakeup call to your own aura.

As if saying, "Hello!!! Would you please dump out that extra STUFF? It never really belonged to you. It came from other people. Don't you have enough to do, dealing with your own STUFF? Lose the extra, already."

Yesterday's assignment, Quality Time With Yourself, helped you practice paying attention to yourself in a deep way, using consciousness.

Be Deep and the Be Deep Quickie also have helped you to direct consciousness toward yourself in a quality way.

Any such technique makes it easier to experience yourself, briefly, in consciousness.

Now your next step is to learn how to move out Imported STUFF from the likes of Lexi.

Having less Imported STUFF in your aura can make it much easier to feel like yourself, act like yourself, be yourself. Even when you're in a room — or talking on your mobile — with somebody else.

That's why the very next thing we'll do together is Wakeup Call.

Wakeup Call

This easy technique clears out Imported STUFF from unskilled empath merges. Clears it out fast.

Doing the Wakeup Call, you'll need to position your awareness in the same direction you have been practicing with Be Deep and related techniques, paying quality attention with consciousness.

Read through the whole recipe first, then cook it!

1. Sit comfortably and close your eyes.
2. Be Deep: Notice what it is like to be you, right now. (No judging, please, just noticing.)
3. Open your eyes enough to read the following sequence of words. Say them out loud:

God, remove from my aura whatever does not belong to me.

Remove from my aura whatever does not belong to me.

Remove from my aura whatever does not belong to me.

Fill me with new love, light, and power.

4. Be Deep: Notice what it is like to be you, right now. (Still no judging allowed! Simply notice whatever you happen to notice.)
5. End the experiment by saying something inside to end the technique, such as "Thank you" or "Experiment complete."
6. Open your eyes.

Now that You're Done, Let's Debrief

Brave Explorer, now that you're out of Technique Time, compare. How did you feel in Step 4, compared to Step 2? Any change would count as an immediate result, right?

When I teach Wakeup Call in a live workshop, most students report some subtle (or not so subtle) improvement, such as feeling:

- Clearer
- More awake inside
- Relaxed
- Calmer
- Less complicated, scattered, or stressed out
- More like "me"

One technique — many possible results. So here's a smart move: From now on, whenever you do Wakeup Call expect nothing. Zilch. Zippo.

Of course, you didn't have this suggestion the first time. So when you were on your own, I wonder. Were you trying to figure out what was (supposedly) supposed to happen? And then make it happen.

Or were you trying to feel a specific result? (That would be something you decided in advance was, supposedly, superior.)

From now on, trust yourself (and me, your teacher) enough to be spontaneous, okay? For one thing, you're co-creating with God. Neither bossing God around nor seeking to obey. This is called CO-CREATION, folks. So you may as well follow the steps of this technique with a certain, very human, kind of innocence.

Yes, Innocence Is Like the "Special Sauce" for This Recipe

So... if you did the Wakeup Call innocently right from the start, congratulations. If not, do it again. And this time, be willing to receive whatever you get.

Ironically, not trying for anything special is the best way to get results from any of the techniques in our 30-Day Plan.

As a bonus, any results you receive can then be valued as things that occurred spontaneously, rather than things you attempted to make happen (perfect for tying yourself up in knots of self-doubt).

Actually, some beginners must do the Wakeup Call several times, doing this on separate occasions, not just repeat-repeat-repeat all in one day (which I never recommend). Eventually they start to notice results.

Hey, this is a 30-Day Plan. Not a 30-Minute Plan, right?

Removing other people's STUFF from your aura causes *subtle* improvement. These are not surface changes, such as you might notice from taking your banged-up car to the body shop.

So if you didn't notice much initially, don't be discouraged. Instead, resolve to be persistent.

Finally, keep in mind that you probably have other kinds of STUFF, not just the Imported kind. How unrealistic it would be to expect this particular technique to remove all the various kinds of STUFF that landed within you long before you met people like Lexi.

Instead, it's wise to seek expert help from people who have learned other skill sets for STUFF identification and removal, such as RES Practitioners. Because we specialize in healing different kinds of energetic STUFF that can impact emotional and spiritual growth.

And, of course, you may find that other sorts of helping-&-and healing professionals fit you better than RES.

What matters? If you feel stuck, choose the kind of help that suits you best!

That said, Imported STUFF is a very big deal for unskilled empaths. So you may be amazed how big a difference the Wakeup Call can make in your life. Starting today.

Your Assignment for Day 5

Easy-peasy. Your assignment for today is simply to use the Wakeup Call three more times. Find out what happens.

In addition, for the rest of this 30-Day Plan, once a day, use the Wakeup Call to clean yourself up.

Afterwards, with more skill, you'll use this technique less frequently. (Eventually, just once a month or less.)

Please hear and understand this: Don't overuse Wakeup Call. It is only *part* of your 30-Day Plan for Empath Empowerment.

DAY 6

The Big Analogy

Have you noticed the difference yet? Every day that you use the techniques and ideas from our 30-Day Plan, you're waking up more from inside. Keep waking up more and more until you are fully awake.

Slap!

Tradition has it that Zen masters sometimes wake up their students by giving them a hit on the head. I'm trying to do something similar, though less painful, through this book.

Of course, your goal isn't necessarily some huge spiritual enlightenment. It's plenty to wake up your consciousness enough to become a skilled empath; awake enough to realize that you can gently position your consciousness wherever you like.

By rights, that is mostly towards yourself... not God or your favorite hobby or whichever random person happens to be in the room along with you.

Learning to pay loving attention to yourself — that is the purpose of experimenting with the Wakeup Call technique from yesterday.

Something similar happens when you sprinkle Be Deep throughout your day. Brave Explorer, you're using the power of your consciousness to become a skilled empath.

The following chapters will continue your progress at becoming self-aware in the way that makes all the difference between life as a skilled empath vs. an unskilled empath, somebody who constantly picks up Imported STUFF from other people and suffers accordingly.

Today's chapter is going to be a bit different. No new techniques to do. Instead, I want to give you something new to just think about. Something big. It's my favorite theory about why empaths suffer so much, and how this suffering is the flip side of something positive.

From Day One

Why were you born as an empath? Was God playing a big game of "Nyah Nyah?" Was the point, "I made you this way on purpose, and My goal was to make you suffer"?

Oh, I don't think so. Instead, let me give you a very bold analogy. An analogy to potty training.

Wouldn't it be convenient if God could have designed humans just a bit differently regarding the human elimination system? How very much nicer would it be if someone like you never needed to do #1 or #2 until you were, say, three years old.

Forget about diapers. One merry morning, when you are ready, Mommy escorts you to the toilet. Then she shows you two interesting new reasons to use it.

Some things, alas, are not possible, not even for God (or your mother). The only way Life's Great Engineer could give you an elimination system was to have it installed and fully functioning right from Day One.

Although this is not one of your proudest childhood stories, chances are that one of your very first acts after birth was to salute your proud mother, the doctor, etc., by sharing your own personal bodily fluids. Messy but absolutely necessary!

Rumor has it, you also demonstrated your vocal power by screaming, crying, etc.

Such a proud moment!

Honestly, what else were you supposed to do with your voice, celebrate your arrival by singing the national anthem? Or maybe you weren't supposed to use your voice at all until ready to say "Please" and "Thank you"?

Wise though you may be as a soul, you weren't born knowing everything. And that includes productive ways to use your empath gift(s).

The gifts of an empath really have plenty in common with pooping. Except that God didn't give empath circuits to everyone, any more than He decided to give everybody cute knees.

But if God did design you as an empath, apparently the only way He could do it was to install your circuits fully switched on, right from birth. Think about it:

- Pooping isn't like talent for playing guitar, developed after you take some lessons.
- Pooping isn't like learning to drive a car, once you are old enough for a learner's permit.
- Pooping is a major, life-long ability, active right from the start.

In these ways, being born as an empath is exactly like being born able to poop. Your lifelong circuits are switched on just as soon as you're born.

Trouble in Eden

Imagine if people had never learned how to control their built-in poop circuits? Suppose that everywhere you went, you'd hear the complaints?

ADAM: Life is so messy.

EVE: I know just what you mean. That smell. It's awful.

ADAM: Well, let's be good sports about it. What else can we do?

EVE: Nothing, I suppose. But at least we can use good manners about this. Honey, never wave your used fig leaves in front of others. Hide them, so that you can develop true dignity.

By Contrast, We've Got It Easy

Luckily for us all, post-postmodern life includes skills for managing those poop circuits. Soon as you're old enough, you learn an excellent skill set called "Potty Training." This gives you control, so you don't keep the ON position going constantly.

Given potty-type skills, you mostly keep those pooping circuits turned OFF, saving up the impulse.

Then, in a chosen place, at whichever time you select, one can consciously choose to turn those circuits fully ON.

And I'll bet you do a fine job of that, too.

Well, folks, that's very much like becoming a skilled empath. So if it cheers you, go forth and consider that "Empath Empowerment" is just a fancy way to say "Potty Training for Empaths."

Although you learned your excellent toilet skills long ago, do you remember? Back in the day, this type of learning involved paying attention to yourself from inside.

Sure, there are social implications of being potty trained. Yet the skill doesn't come from having Aunt Myrtle follow you around for the rest of your life, asking every five minutes, "Dear, do you have to go to the big kid's room now?"

For both skill sets, the source of control lies within you. Rest assured, if you were coordinated enough to learn potty training back in the day, then you're fully capable of becoming a skilled empath now.

Your Assignment for Day 6

Today, think about our fun little analogy. Not obsessively, and not just the potty part. Remember occasionally that, of course, you can use your own consciousness circuits to pay attention to yourself as The Most Important Person in the Room.

Just because someone else happens to be in the room to distract you, must you lose bladder control? Well, it's exactly the same with your empath circuits.

Paying attention to yourself as the main person — that can become your habit. No need to sit in the midst of a party wearing a forced expression, until it's so obvious you're straining that Aunt Myrtle must grab you by the elbow, forcibly escorting you to that very special room.

You can afford to be natural about empath skills, just like your (by now) totally routine toilet training.

For the empath's version, have fun by being yourself. Noticing others, sure. But keep bringing attention back to yourself:

- What's interesting to you right now.
- Your ideas and opinions.
- Your desires.
- How you plan to use your time right now.
- Yep, all about me-me-me.

In terms of consciousness, you can use a couple of the cool skills you've already learned.

A few times today, experiment with Be Deep.

And do Wakeup Call once.

Mostly, though, pay attention to yourself in that quality way, Brave Explorer: as though you're The Most Important Person in the Room. By tomorrow, you'll be ready to graduate to Part Two of Empath Empowerment.

Becoming a Skilled Empath

PART TWO

Strengthen Your Way of Being You

What happens when you feel and act like The Most Important Person in the Room? The difference is symbolized in the picture opposite, where "You" are fully in focus while others fade into the background.

As The Most Important Person in The Room, you can still get along with others, and do it as someone who is compassionate, kind and thoughtful. But you can also do this while keeping your empath gift(s) turned firmly OFF.

Must you keep living this way for the rest of your life? Of course not. After completing our 30-Day Plan — even during Part Three of this Plan — sometimes you will choose to turn your gift(s) ON.

In every case, however, that can be a choice. Quite a contrast to the habit of an unskilled empath, which is to keep each gift perpetually turned all the way ON!

Boldly break your old habit of doing unskilled empath merges. Instead, experiment with how you hold a space. Mostly pay attention to yourself — which is what healthy non-empaths always do, and without working at it.

Putting yourself first, you'll make subtle shifts that direct your consciousness. This is not the same thing as trying to manipulate your personality or social boundaries.

These subtle shifts of consciousness won't seem fake. They won't hurt anyone. Techniques that I share with you in Part Two will be for your private exploration.

Other folks won't disappear. Or be hurt. Probably they won't even notice.

Body Day

"Stop taking on random Imported STUFF from others."

In practice, what does that mean? You start a new kind of experiment; it's called becoming The Most Important Person in the Room.

Different from "Boundaries"

As I introduce you to this new phase of your Empath Empowerment training, please note the context. We are NOT having a conversation about social behavior. Boundaries are NOT what we're exploring.

Boundaries involve behavior. Toddlers, for instance, have a strong sense of boundaries. Everything is "Mine."

We grownups are different because we learn manners. Sometimes we learn manners so well that, whether empaths or non-empaths, we forget our appropriate social boundaries.

Then we need Psychology Talk, such as:

- "No, you don't have to give your nice coat away, just because somebody else admires it."
- "If you've been mixing up your needs with the needs of other people, stop."

Good advice to be sure! Nonetheless, social-level advice is quite irrelevant to our skill set. This 30-Day Plan involves waking up consciousness from inside yourself.

Mastering this, learning many approaches and developing finesse with your own consciousness — this can help you to form new habits about how you treat yourself. Changes to social behavior, if needed, will develop automatically. Do first things first.

Empaths have a tendency to identify strongly with being other people. Hannah's back pain becomes your pain. Lexi's longing for friendship becomes your longing. And you already know how much fun that is!

When you become The Most Important Person in the Room, what *doesn't* happen? Being in the room with other people, you don't automatically drift into identifying with them. One way to break that habit is to make today (and part of every day) Body Day.

The Pinch of Life

Imagine that you've drifted off to sleep. Or maybe not. Hmm, you're not sure.

What's a quick 'n easy way to tell? Pinch yourself.

Hey, I can't take credit for inventing this technique, but it's still a good one for our skill set.

If awake, one pinch will give you the familiar and unmistakable sensation of being in your physical body. If dreaming, a pinch can't duplicate that sensation.

I call it "The Pinch of Life," as in "Human Life When Wide Awake" and "Life in My Physical Body."

Give yourself a pinch if you start drifting into the experience of being another person in the room.

Say that you're with Troy, star forward among the neighborhood soccer guys, a person of immense prestige and fascination. He's describing his latest triumph doing a hat trick, and you're just enthralled, listening and (without trying to, consciously) supporting him with your auric energy.

Eventually, you will have a moment of choice. This will be subtle, not like hearing a referee blow a whistle and scream:

"Red card." Instead, you'll realize something like:
"I'm getting so involved in listening to Troy. Maybe it's time to go back to making *myself* The Most Important Person in The Room."

Give yourself a quick pinch, on the hand or somewhere even less conspicuous. As if to remind yourself:

Hello! I'm alive in my own body and I know it!

Usually, that's all it takes for you to resume your rightful place as The Most Important Person in The Room. If not, add the Be Deep Quickie.

Here comes the really wild part. After you do The Pinch, will Troy notice the difference? Probably not! Assuming that he's a non-empath, he's used to feeling like The Most Important Person in The Room. Troy will do just fine. While you will get to feel like *you*.

Whenever you realize that you have a choice about being The Most Important Person in The Room, wake yourself up, even if you have to use a little pinch to do so.

Notice, you never need ask permission before shifting attention back to yourself. Moving your consciousness is not like elementary school, where you had to raise your hand for approval before you could go to the water fountain. Move your consciousness freely whenever you like.

Got a Problem with That?

Sometimes we empaths fear that if they withdraw the support of their consciousness, other people will crumble like a harshly treated saltine. If you're worrying, please answer the following questions:

- Will other people really die without having me as their version of life support?

- Then how do they manage when I'm not physically present?
- Might they also have been created with an inner consciousness?
- Might each person, not just me, possess a vital link to God that can be used as a source of supply?
- Did God make all other people super-fragile, while I am the only strong one?
- Is there really any grown-up on earth who depends on being nurtured by my consciousness and personal energy?
- Why?

Brave Explorer, Let's Get Real

If the problem isn't actually other people's fragility, then what? Maybe, just maybe, the true problem comes down to enabling.

As you may know, ENABLING means protecting someone, like an alcoholic, from the consequences of his or her own problems.

By enabling, maybe you help that person short-term.

However, what are you achieving long-term? Only keeping him/her stuck in a limiting pattern.

Besides that, here's a thought experiment you might do, just for giggles. Assume that Troy is so energetically feeble that he must always cling to others energetically. Where is it written that the person depended upon must be *you*?

If you stop volunteering to supplying your energy, can't the Troy's of the world still manage to survive?

Hint: What, you think you're the only empath on earth? If Troy wants to find an empath enabler, he can. Although you're special, if someone seeks the short-term relief of another person's unskilled empath merges… other empaths can be found, right?

Cool Extras

During Body Day, it's helpful to know many ways to wake up your physical awareness. Here are other skills that I like. Check them out and see if you find any of them to be helpful.

1. Feel your heartbeat or touch the pulse on your wrist. Is it slow and steady? Scared and rabbit-like? Explore.
2. Find the nearest mirror. Take a look at yourself. Even if other people nearby are reflected there, you can find yourself, right? It's a good objective reminder that you *are* in the room in the first place. This will make it easier to consider yourself The Most Important Person in The Room.
3. Rub two fingers together, like thumb and forefinger. Doing this very discretely can remind you, "Hey, I'm here."
4. Even more secretly, wiggle your toes.

Your Assignment for Day 7

Celebrate your body today, Brave Explorer. Celebrate by paying your body some positive attention.

Do this however and wherever you like, within reason. How often will you choose to pay attention to your physical self? That's nobody else's business.

Body Day is a vital part of your skill set for Empath Empowerment.

Still, it is just one part. So, please, if somebody demands that you summarize your 30-Day Plan in 30 seconds, for pity's sake, don't say, "All you have to do is wiggle your toes."

DAY 8

Mind Day

Paying attention to yourself yesterday, rather than the Troy's and Lexi's of the world, did you notice? Nobody died. Empaths tend to support others constantly with awareness. You may not realize you're doing this until you stop for a while. Then you get it. Now let's help you get it even better.

Empath's Pantomime

Other people probably need way less support than you have been giving them. Here's a way to prove this to yourself. It's a pair exercise I developed for a workshop.

For this version you will need a partner, but this other person doesn't have to be an empath, merely somebody who is both alive, human, and willing to play a silly game with you.

When you're going to do the exercise and not just read about it, find that volunteer. Stand opposite each other.

You'll be taking turns, Brave Explorer. First time around, one of you plays The Leader, while the other will act as The Follower. Second time around, switch. Here's what to do.

1. For two minutes, The Leader moves slowly into different positions, changing the angles of arms, legs, head, etc.
2. The Follower's job is to copy the Leader's motions, like a pantomime artist.
3. After you're done playing both roles, discuss what this exercise was like for each of you, being The Leader and also being The Follower.

Now Let's Debrief

Of course, only read this section after you have done the Empath's Pantomime. Otherwise you will spoil it as a first-time learning experience.

When You Were The Follower

Brave Explorer, were you inwardly trying to make things nice for The Leader?

Remember, your job was to copy The Leader's movements. That simple. But, besides doing that, were you also sending out a supportive kind of caring? For instance, you could have been giving nonverbal cues like "I'm ready now for your next move"?

When You Were The Leader

This time, were you trying to make things nice for The Follower? That might include making sure the tempo was suitable, not doing anything too challenging, etc. Instead of focusing mostly on leading during this exercise, did you focus at least as much on helping your partner to do the job of following you?

The first time I assigned this exercise in a workshop, I asked my Pantomime Artists if this had been the case. Some got it right away and started to laugh. Others skeptically said, "Nooooooooooooooooo."

So I told them, "Prove it" The whole group was instructed to repeat the exercise, only this time to keep it simple. "If you lead, just lead. If you follow, just follow. Later, we'll discuss your experiences."

Were those skeptics ever surprised! Doing their second round of Empath's Pantomime, they realized they *had* been doing a lot with their consciousness, far more than they noticed. Why? Supportive volunteer work had been an unquestioned habit.

A habit? Yes, merely a habit.

That habit of supporting others with your consciousness is the habit we're about to change, Brave Explorers. Starting now. This silly habit corresponds to merging your aura with people for no good reason, except that they happen to be in the room with you.

Focus on yourself from now on, okay? Keep things simple. You could even call it "Keep things surface."

And if you have a partner nearby, do a second round of Empath's Pantomime, putting yourself first, you, The Most Important Person in the Room.

How to Celebrate Mind Day

Taking self-awareness further, let's consider what it means to *use your mind*. This contrasts to what most empaths do on a daily basis, which is to *lose your mind*.

Why lose your mind? Because you're so busy sharing it with everyone else.

What is your mind, anyway? By definition (and meaning no insult) your mind is surprisingly simple. Not simple-minded, just human. Here's a success story that illustrates how your simple human mind can lead to triumph.

No Traffic Accidents for 2 Million Miles

Deb Davis is a long haul truck driver for Frito-Lay. After 26 years, she won an award from the company for driving two million miles without an accident. Deb lives in Wisconsin, which gets its share of snow. But she's never had a traffic accident at work. Neither has she ever had a car crash.

What is the secret of Deb's perfect driving record? She was asked this during an interview on the National Public Radio show "All Things Considered."

Deb's answer? "Paying attention."

Driving is "very, very simple," according to Deb Davis. She explained that if she ever got in an accident it would mean that she wasn't doing what she was supposed to be doing as a driver, paying attention.

According to Ms. Davis, life is very simple if you let it be. What makes this award-winning driver so special? Maybe it's just that she uses her mind.

Choosing Your Mind. Using Your Mind.

To be human means that you have both a simple mind and a complex intellect. Tomorrow will be Intellect Day. By contrast, today is Mind Day, where you get to explore the glories of your mind and how that trusty mind of yours can help with Empath Empowerment.

What's the difference between mind and intellect? Telling the difference can seem tricky at first, since your mind and intellect both function by means of thoughts. But with your mind, thoughts involve concepts that you've already mastered. For instance:

- Point to 10 different things in the place where you are right now, counting out loud as you go.
- Name 10 different colors in the place where you are right now, saying the name of each color out loud.
- Which are you doing right now, swimming or reading? You can't be doing both. Because you are human, your mind allows you to do just one thing, at a time.

For humans, using your mind is a way to do only one thing at a time, and do it with singular focus: Chop wood. Carry water.

Drink the water. Don't try drinking the wood.

Granted, if you were God, your mind might work differently. But, with all respect, when was the last time anyone called you omniscient?

Being human, whenever you wish, you can favor this simple-minded version of reality called "the mind." To wake up your mind, list out loud whatever you're doing, one thing at a time, one thought at a time.

Mindfulness can be very soothing. It can create a kind of mini-eternity, only set in the present. While you're being mindful, it's impossible to rush. As one of my students put it, "All the busy-ness goes away when I enter the practical Mind."

Who's in Charge of Your Mind, Anyway?

It's you, of course. You're in charge… even if another person happens to be in the room with you. You're in charge… even if you used to have the habit of treating that other person like The Most Important Person in the Room.

Habits or no habits, you've never truly relinquished control. Potentially at least, you always have been in control of your mind.

To stay in control more consistently, make one simple choice in the here and now. Know that you're the one who chooses where you'll direct your attention. This doesn't "just happen." At least, that's not how it has to be for you from now on.

For example, suppose that you speak English but you have also managed to learned another language, Swahili. Great!

Next, imagine that you're walking down the street, talking with a friend, and busily thinking away in English.

Does it ever happen that Swahili randomly takes you over and suddenly, it's just got to be all Swahili, all the time?

Of course not. Assuming that you are sane, you get to choose. Speaking an extra language doesn't mean switching tongues for no reason.

You are the one in control of your languages. Likewise, you are also in control of your mind. Which brings us to your assignment for today, Brave Explorer.

Sharpen Your Mind

There's a story I want you to tell yourself. It's the story of your life, as experienced with your mind.

Nothing intimidating here. Just supply a short play-by-play commentary for a minute, out loud.

Observe the surface facts, just the facts.

Automatically, this will shift attention to your mind. And the more you talk in this way, the easier it gets. Until you could talk about surface things forever.

For example:

> *I'm in the room with Roscoe.*
>
> *Now I hear him speak.*
>
> *Roscoe is speaking Swahili.*
>
> *I'm sitting on the sofa.*
>
> *As I look around, I notice that this room has additional furniture, and it also has a floor and a ceiling.*
>
> *Now I hear the sound of clinking. It comes from the ice cubes in my glass of soda.*
>
> *I am holding this glass. I am holding it up to my lips.*
>
> *I raise my lower lip and tilt the glass.*
>
> *Liquid moves from the glass into my body.*
>
> *There is a taste of Coca-Cola.*

Nothing fancy here, right? Yet telling this mind-level story is balm to your mind.

Whenever you speak your surface story out loud, that positions your consciousness firmly in that inner category called "Mind."

Thinking that story will do the same thing, as long as you're not multi-tasking. (Multi-tasking automatically brings awareness to the intellect.)

When you do this technique, I'm recommending that you do the narration out loud to help you become totally focused and clear, sharpening your mind.

Choosing to be report on life from the perspective of your mind, for your sole benefit — liberating! This helps you to become The Most Important Person in The Room. Specifically, this is one more way to turn your human sense of self ON, while turning your empath's gift(s) OFF.

Some Story! Does It Enthrall You?

"Golly," you may be thinking. "An awful lot of people today must have very sharp minds because they're constantly talking drivel, like on their mobile phones. As if everybody within earshot really needs to be informed, "I am here. I am standing outside. I am calling you and it is two o'clock."

Yes, people around you often say the obvious, frequently saying it with great enthusiasm, and often sharing their equally obvious comments in other ways. By tweeting. By liking. Or by sending you "clever" posts on Facebook that are thuddingly obvious.

Many of these annoying news reports *sound* just like what you've just done today. However, that doesn't make them serve the same purpose as Sharpen Your Mind. Remember, I'm inviting you to do that in order to purposely position consciousness at the level of your mind. This exercise is to be done privately. Call it a "Mindfulness Technique" if you like, only please do it gently.

Why "gently"? Since I've observed that, sadly, some fans of mindfulness do a heavy-handed, way-overthinking, self-conscious version. Not just sitting on the sofa." But adding thoughts, like "I. Am. Being. Aware. Of myself, sitting... on THE SooooHFaH."

Please, please, never mess with your mind in that way. (And if you want details, just book a personal session with me. I'll research an energetic hologram of your own aura, dating from a time when you did this icky kind of thing to yourself. After I describe the impact on your aura and subconscious mind, very likely, you'll never want to "improve" yourself in that kind of way… ever again.

Alternatively, you can simply say no. Mindfulness? Yes. Overbearing, Show-Offey Mindfulness? No, no, no.

Using Your Mind Never Has to Be Obnoxious

Trust this Empath Coach. Just as you can easily opt out of show-offey mindfulness techniques, trust that you won't somehow get stuck in Perpetual Mind Day. Not as a result of today's experiment!

As for those people in your life who constantly talk about the surface of life as if there were no alternative? Using your mind a bit more won't reduce you to their way of talking. Incidentally, those folks you know who are enthralled with reporting on the surface of life — chances are, they're not empaths like you.

Besides, another factor may be that they overuse their minds because they don't use their intellects much. (Tomorrow, of course, will be our official Intellect Day. Even before then, most likely you're in no danger of living like all mind, no intellect.)

Also, in case you're wondering, using social media or mobile phones to broadcast whatever crosses one's mind? This does not necessarily involve waking up within oneself, nor does it come remotely close to becoming a skilled empath.

Therefore, in our Plan there is no Twitter Day. But there is definitely Mind Day. And you can have yours. Starting now.

Your Assignment for Day 8

Three different times today, speak out loud for 2-5 minutes, speaking in the manner of Mind Day. Nothing impressive. Just stating the obvious.

Obvious? No worries! Obviousness is the glory of Mind Day.

DAY 9

Intellect Day

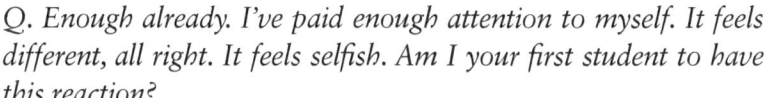

Q. *Enough already. I've paid enough attention to myself. It feels different, all right. It feels selfish. Am I your first student to have this reaction?*

A. No, it's pretty common during the process of gaining Empath Empowerment. Paying so much attention to yourself, all kinds of doubts can arise.

Your intellect is dominating now, or you wouldn't be circling around with self-doubt. Let's emphasize your intellect's strengths, since it's so active.

Intellect is the category of yourself that you depend upon to evaluate things like "when have I done enough?" Intellect drives decision-making. Creativity, too.

Yesterday, Mind Day, you had ample opportunity to make yourself The Most Important Person in the Room by enjoying simple pleasures, like naming different colors around you.

Choosing not to let your consciousness slide into identifying with other people, you used your mind to gently bring attention back to yourself in present surroundings.

If your mind were a game, it would be *Bingo* or *Lotto*. By contrast, your intellect (today's focus for exploration) is more like *Scrabble* or *Chess*. Your intellect is also required for that wildly popular post-modern game called "*Multi-Tasking.*"

Q. Ha! I can prove you wrong. Say that my multi-tasking involves listening to music and eating my lunch. Why would my intellect be involved at all?

A. Your intellect plays the role of traffic director. When your hand goes to turn up the volume of that music, it doesn't reach for your mouth. Nor do you squish a spoonful of mashed potatoes into your sound equipment. (I'm hoping.)

Even if you are loving the food, and you only play music in the background for setting a mood to enhance the meal, what has been kissed goodbye? It's spontaneous, healthy awareness of your physical body.

Because you are playing that music, what has been put in charge? It's your intellect, which now must switch back and forth between the food and the music, maybe your emotions as well, deciding which category to favor when.

Q. Okay, then. But I already know what you're going to assign us for today. It's going to be like yesterday, only using the intellect. Boring!

Besides, what would make that different, really different, from spending my day doing some psychological exercise about protecting my boundaries?

A. Such a good question! It deserves a good-sized answer, even its very own heading....

Resistance

For mastery at turning your empath gift(s) OFF, you must be able to direct your consciousness toward every category of your human equipment. Admittedly, you'll use only one category at a time. But it's best to keep every category available. There are, after all, only seven: Mind, body, spirit, intellect, soul, emotions and environment.

By hook or by crook or by taking a look, you are developing skill with them all. Flexibility for shifting awareness is vital for Empath Empowerment. So is freedom. A special kind of freedom is yours when can you experience life through every one of these seven categories.

During this second part of our 30-Day Plan, yes, you're opening up the fullest awareness possible of each category. There's no substitute, not if you aim to develop a complete set of skills as an empath.

To become just a semi-skilled empath, you could get by with three or four categories. Yet wouldn't you prefer to develop the full skill set? Especially because, in doing so, you will become more self-actualized as a person! For that, you'll need to learn how to activate awareness at every single category available to you as a human being, the entire set of seven. Which has nothing to do with boundaries. And everything to do with using your consciousness appropriately.

Well, what's to keep you from doing that? **RESISTANCE**. It can come up any day during our 30-Day Plan.

Should you feel resistance, consider the context. What was happening right before you started to feel that resistance?

Sometimes the very idea of playing with one category of your human self becomes a huge turn-off. Resistance will bring you feelings like "I don't wanna."

Actually, resistance can come in a thousand variations. For example, my questioner in today's chapter expressed resistance to paying attention to herself and then to using her intellect. It was Meg, actually. And if only you could have heard her tone of voice while asking these questions!

Normally Meg seems meek as could be. Just between you and me, this time her attitude really shocked me. She sounded arrogant and defensive.

That's fine with me, so long as she doesn't quit but follows our 30-Day Plan all the way through.

How about you? Have you encountered resistance yet, whether during Body Day or Mind Day or any other part of our 30-Day Plan? Let's do some problem solving. What can you do if you start feeling that you just hate exploring some part of your human identity, such as your intellect?

Four choices are listed below. The first two could be called "bad," but they're also "popular" and "very understandable." Seems to me, the last two choices will serve you much better, especially in the long run. You're the one who decides, though.

1. Blame

What if you dislike experiencing one of the components of your human self, such as your body, mind, intellect? Positioning awareness there might make you feel bored, trivialized, empty, sad, or scared.

Well, you could always try blaming. Rant about life or your childhood or how the way Rose is teaching you through this book. Although blame doesn't really fix problems, it can be fun... and make you feel superior to whatever you blame.

2. Escape

Whenever you encounter a dead spot within your own feelings, surely you can find ways to distract yourself. If you don't like using your mind, body, intellect, etc., don't. For instance, you could live in your spirituality instead.

Many people do. And they're considered perfectly sane. (Marginally sane, anyway. Self-actualizing, however? No.)

Escaping can seem like the simplest possible solution. But it reminds me of Ethel, a woman I knew in college who didn't like eating vegetables.

At age 20, she resolved that henceforth she would never eat a vegetable again. Problem solved. In a way.

You could have a pretty good life despite hating and ignoring components of yourself, but I guarantee you'll have a better life by making your peace with them.

3. Just Keep on Doing Your Silly Techniques

Let's say that you don't enjoy doing one of the techniques from our 30-Day Plan. Instead of escape or blaming, you could go back and do that technique again and again. Continue doing it once a day until you stop resisting it.

For instance, say that you hated doing the exercise to "Sharpen Your Mind." In this case, out of self-love (not masochism) you could repeat Mind Day. You could stretch your personal growth even further by doing Mind Week.

Meaning what? Every day for that week, you would keep on playing with mindfulness a few times daily, undeterred by resistance. Any time your own mind seems scary, you can give that resistance a big, loud "Ha, ha, ha." Then return to that same technique, just for a minute or so. Then consider yourself wildly successful, both at practicing the technique and at melting resistance.

Yes, a relentless approach like this can melt resistance away. Provided that you treat yourself lovingly, not punitively. Soon, you'll become a person who likes your own mind or body or whatever.

4. Seek Appropriate Professional Help

Once upon a time, some of my students had pretty severe resistance to experiencing to their own minds, emotions, etc. They weren't crazy, more like what psychologists call "the worried well."

Some chose to do healing sessions with me, where I helped them move STUFF out of their auras through sessions of RES Energy HEALING. Afterwards they moved forward much faster at Empath Empowerment.

Other clients were more comfortable seeing a psychotherapist or some other resource for getting unstuck. Which kind of help would you seek, if stuck? That's entirely up to you.

What if you find yourself battling any aspect of yourself, and it's way hard? Please be kind to yourself. Seek help from a professional who seems right for you. Professional services can save enormous amounts of time and frustration, so don't be cheap with yourself.

Fact is, do-it-yourself efforts work only up to a point. A professional could save you years of struggle against resistance. In fact, you might need just a session or two and ta da! You're unstuck.

Now Let's Wake Up Your Intellect

Brave Explorer, we've dealt with resistance (in theory, at least). Now let's explore Intellect Day. I'll share with you four different techniques that can help you to wake up your intellect. (All are to be used in your personal life only, not while you're at work.)

To liven up each technique, I'll supply examples by bringing in various buddies from our Cast of Characters.

Intellect Aid #1. Depth Probe

This is a technique to use while you're interacting with someone else, especially being together in the same room.

Use your intellect to define how deeply you need to be involved in the relationship.

While you're with James, for instance, take a few seconds (only) to think about questions like these:

- "What is James literally saying here? Is there a subtext that I'm noticing to the point where I ignore his actual words?"
- "Is James asking me to help him in any way or is he simply talking?"

∽ Whatever answer you receive, accept it. Then return to engaging fully in your conversation.

Have you guessed? The point of this silent inquiry is simply to switch on your intellect.

Might you learn something from the Depth Probe that causes you to make changes in how you relate to your friend?

Sure, but that's optional, just an extra benefit of doing the technique. Even if you don't change a thing about how you interact with James, just by doing the Depth Probe, you win.

Victory means this: You have used your intellect to wake up from inside.

Just bear in mind, Brave Explorer, easy does it. Depth Probe is best used for only a few seconds at a time. You question. You answer. Then return to the conversation.

Only a few seconds — that's very important. The goal of Empath Empowerment is a natural state. Comfortably living on the human-friendly surface of life, living as The Most Important Person in The Room.

Introducing Our Next Intellect Aid

Before learning our next intellect-friendly, technique, here come some questions. When you're with other adults, is your first loyalty to them or to yourself?

1. If they asked you to donate an arm, you might not think twice. But what if you were asked to give them major chunks of your consciousness?
2. In fact, what if you have been volunteering to do this in ways that haven't been necessary?

Hey, as The Most Important Person in the Room, you can habitually put yourself first, and do this without appearing grotesquely conceited.

Suppose that you're in a room with James and the rest of the cocktail party. Are you really enjoying your conversation with him? If not, remember this saying: *So many men, so little time!*

While with him, you can allow your head to swivel occasionally, noticing other available people... or anything else in the room that you might prefer to notice... instead of that likeable but sleep-inducing James.

How often have you passively waited for another person to end a conversation? Is the purpose of relationships really to be of service to others until they have sucked you dry?

Yet sometimes it isn't socially appropriate to do a head swivel, followed by a heel swivel, and blurt out "Buh-Bye" to well meaning James. When you're stuck, use our next technique, Cocktail Party.

In this next technique, your intellect helps you to question reality, very helpful if you must stay put. I call it "Cocktail Party" because these light-hearted social events are famous for fickleness. Heads swivel freely. Once a conversation turns even slightly boring, suave cocktail party guests will offer a flimsy excuse and scamper away. Starting today, you can do a version of this while staying put.

Intellect Aid #2. Cocktail Party

That's how it's done, Dahling. These events don't have to be taken seriously. You're not consulting with the Delphic Oracle. You're only hanging out at a silly cocktail party.

While talking with James, at any random time, remember your inner freedom of movement. So often, an empath doesn't play anything remotely resembling "Cocktail Party."

Before today, even if you literally were at a cocktail party, would you scamper away when bored? Heavens no. More likely you acted as though locked in a confessional — on the priest's side — possibly stuck there for hours.

By contrast, this Cocktail Party technique gives you permission to scamper more and suffer less. And never worry that exercising freedom of choice makes you "bad."

Move away inwardly, that's all. Pay only enough attention to James so that you can nod your head appropriately when he pauses his monologue. Otherwise indulge in your own thoughts, feelings, physical sensations, etc. Let your intellect act as "The Switcher."

In short, when it comes to social situations that you're obligated to go through, even without much enthusiasm, you really can do Cocktail Party. Why continue to pay close attention to every random person who crosses your path? Consider yourself liberated. If it helps, think of it this way:

You're not being rude by not staying glued.

Our next technique will add a bit of contrast. Rather than opting OUT somewhat, you can choose to opt IN.

Intellect Aid #3. Insisting

In the midst of talking to strangers or friends, you do have the right to enjoy yourself. Well, insist upon that. Suppose you're talking with Roscoe. When in doubt about having fun, use your intellect to pose this very useful question: "Am I having fun right now?"

If you're enjoying Roscoe' company, go with the flow.

If you're *not* having fun, and it's socially acceptable to leave, end that conversation and leave.

What if you're not having a great time but duty requires that you stay there with Roscoe? Somehow you can still find a way to have fun. Use your intellect as a tool for secret enjoyment.

Intellect can be great for that. Your intellect offers countless ways to slice, dice or chop your reality, helping you to notice whatever you find interesting.

Incidentally, can that include using that clever intellect of yours to ask some questions? Sure.

Yes, you're allowed to secretly use that intellect wherever you happen to be. When you insist on enjoying yourself, your intellect can help make it happen.

I remember reading an interview with Jodie Foster, a brilliant woman, a Yale grad and, also, an actress since childhood. Jodie has spent long periods of time hanging around movie sets. So the interviewer asked how she coped with the boredom.

How did Jodie answer? "I've never been bored in my life."

Now, there's a person who knows how to use her intellect. Sound like you to you? If not, you can become that kind of person.

Of Course, Your Intellect Can Bring You Great Fun

So can your mind, your body, or other components of yourself that we'll be exploring in days to come.

What happens when you insist upon having fun? First of all, know it's allowed. You have every right to live juicy. So, using your intellect, choose to pay attention however you like, such as:

- Ask questions that would make the conversation become more interesting
- Listen to the quality of voices, the underlying silence, whichever sounds are within earshot
- Find your favorite colors in the room. Explore how they look
- Compare and contrast the shapes of nearby objects as though you were an artist
- Silently do face readings on others in the room.

Yes, you can do your duty yet still find a way to have fun.

Actually, that's one way to understand what it means, being The Most Important Person in The Room: You're allowed to have plenty of fun!

Intellect Aid #4. Transferable Email Skill

Just because you've got mail, must you scrutinize every message word for word? That way, you'd never leave your computer. *You* might start to feel like spam, due to reading so much of it.

Surely you have developed survival skills for dealing with spam. Even genuine emails where your friend Jocelyn describes her latest pedicure in thrilling detail! Just because messages fill up your in-box doesn't mean you're required to read every word.

What if Zachary happens to be in the room with you, rather than your in-box? Hey, you're still in charge of message management.

Should Zachary seem annoyingly intense, or unbelievably boring, you can treat him like spam. Inwardly press "delete."

In human terms, what does it mean to stay in a social situation after you press "delete"? Brave Explorer, you're allowed to just go through the motions.

When someone sends you an email that you don't like for any reason, you know how to treat that email. Just because someone stands before you in 3-D, why should that inner power diminish?

How appropriate that Intellect Day would be packed with four new techniques! Any one of them can help you to relish your discerning, delightful, direct-able intellect.

Do remember, Brave Explorer, that today's adventures are only part of Empath Empowerment, not the whole thing.

Because I don't want you to be tempted to overuse intellectual games. Ideally, you'll use what you've learned today as just part of your 3-D, 30-Day Plan for Empath Empowerment.

Your Assignment for Day 9

Today's assignment is to playfully use your intellect as a means to make yourself The Most Important Person in the Room.

As with previous days, I'm not suggesting that you go into a long-detached state. Simply use your intellect *on purpose, briefly* and *occasionally*. Let it help you to make your experience of life to become more stimulating, intellectually.

Choose any our four techniques for today. Or make up new techniques of your own, designed to switch on your intellect.

DAY 10

Emotions Day

Saddle up, cowboys and cowgirls. You have a big herd to tend today. Those "cattle" are your emotions. Notice them grazing free over the plains: Large cows, little calves, and the occasional frolicsome bull. Each one is named after an emotion, like *Humperdinck the Melancholy*. And they're all yours.

So herd those cows today, because emotions are another self-category that a skilled empath must be able to identify.

Am I suggesting that you spend all day contemplating your astrological chart, your navel, or that large spotted animal down yonder named *Bessie, Who Languishes Due to Frustrated Rebelliousness?*

Heck, no. You're just doing the same basic moves as you did on Body Day, Mind Day or Intellect Day. Gently you're paying occasional attention to this chosen category of your mind-body-spirit-intellect-soul-emotions-environment.

Quick Emotional Upgrade

Ah, emotions. My emotions!
If ever you find yourself caught up in emotions belonging to others — their problems, their thinking, their religious conflicts, their fears about the environment; emotions of any kind, even mild jealousy over "Ooh, Zachary's fantastic hairstyle" — what can you do about it?

1. **Start with a round of Be Deep. You are you, not anyone else.**

2. Soon as possible, use your Wakeup Call to clear out your aura. (Really, it's no bigger a deal than blowing your nose. Only you'll use a few well chosen words rather than tissues.)
3. Immediately afterwards, pay attention to your emotions for a few seconds.

That simple, you Brave Explorers! So there's a start! Next, let's turn to some extra skills I like to call...

Herding and Branding

Whenever you find yourself straying into other people's inner experiences, instead of your own, *Whoa buckaroo, don't you have some herding to do?*

Personally, I think that branding an animal is disgusting. Imagine having a searing hot iron pushed into *your* flesh, just so you can proudly wear the name of some ranch, like "The Lazy Overachiever." However we'll be doing a mere thought experiment. Our "brand" won't be a hot piece of metal, more like a slogan. And using it should never produce a smell like some panicked, sweaty animal.

Really, it can be quite simple to claim your own emotions and find them more interesting than emotions belonging to other people. Stopping to notice emotions at depth counts for Technique Time. And I do recommend that you give yourself just 20 Daily Minutes of Technique Time, Tops.

All the rest of your waking hours, live like the human you are. Neither analyzing at depth. Nor meditating. Nor confusing emotions with The Cosmic Meaning Of Life.

Brand Your Cattle

This technique is designed to help you stop living in a way that overemphasizes emotions. If you start wallowing in emotions while on your own — or if you start wallowing in other people's emotions while you're with them, stop it.

To stop it, brand those emotions (or cattle) for what they are. Say the following words out loud. What if it would be socially awkward to say them? Then think them.

> *Right now, I choose to pay attention to emotions on a surface level. This is becoming my new habit — my new default.*
>
> *When I notice emotions belonging to others, it's enough to notice them just on the surface. My default!*
>
> *And the same with my own emotions. Automatically I notice them right on the surface. My default!*
>
> *But what if I wish to pay deeper attention to my emotions? Or anyone else's? Sure I can. But that's an exception to my usual way of dealing with emotions. I may choose to emphasize deep emotions — or anything else I like — during each day's official Technique Time, 20 minutes total. That's it.*
>
> *Otherwise I hereby brand my emotions. They're "Just emotions." Part of my life. Not all of my life.*

After you go through these words, return to being "a normal person." Say things. Do things. Including how you talk with other people: Not talking to their deep emotions. Simply talking to people as if they were people. (Which, actually, they are.)

You see, Brave Explorers, on Emotions Day, you won't have to use the "Brand Your Cattle" technique constantly. Please do not think that you have just received a set of magical words, so all you need do is repeat them incessantly and you will become a skilled empath.

This new Brand Your Cattle technique is only one part of your skill set for Empath Empowerment. Especially useful if, as an empath, you have the gift of Emotional Intuition or Emotional Oneness or both. But Brand Your Cattle will help you as an empath, regardless of whichever empath gift(s) you have. Including none that are emotional in nature.

Use this technique at will to point your consciousness away from emotions and back in the direction called "Objective Reality." Life around you! Effectiveness at life! Yes, human-type results. And this is just part of becoming The Most Important Person in The Room.

Not only can this technique become a useful part of Emotions Day. So can the general idea of *paying attention to emotions right on the surface*. Does that mean you will never enjoy that interesting experience of doing a Skilled Empath Merge? Of course not.

As a skilled empath, sometimes you'll choose to turn your gift(s) ON. We will get to that later in our 30-Day Plan. Promise! Meanwhile, I don't want to alarm you but, for most of my students, a healthy ratio of Empath OFF to Empath ON is about 600:2.

That's right, as a graduate of our 30-Day Plan, you'll average spending 600 minutes, or 10 hours, on yourself… before lavishing 2 minutes on somebody else, when using the mighty power of your consciousness. Thus, doing Skilled Empath Merge quite sparingly.

Is that fair? Sure — fair to you, Brave Explorer.

To be effective at helping others, as well as effective at maintaining your sanity, empaths need to turn their gift(s) firmly OFF most of the time. Surely I don't have to remind you of our lovely analogy about potty training….

Name Those Cute Little Cows

What will happen today as you turn ON surface awareness of your emotions and those emotions of other people? (And turn OFF the deep part.) Regarding other people, a better way to make contact with their feelings is to use "Emotional Intelligence."

This useful concept was developed by Daniel Goleman, Ph.D., author of a bestselling book called *Emotional Intelligence*. The brilliant Dr. Goleman, and his aura, are living proof that a person can develop superb skill at Emotional Intelligence without being an empath.

To simplify Goleman's important discovery, Emotional Intelligence requires that you name emotions belonging to others as well as yourself, then get a sense of social politics between people and act appropriately to fit in. Emotions show in tone of voice, facial expression, body language, as well as the actual words being spoken out loud.

Anyone can learn Emotional Intelligence. It's actually a way to use your mind (i.e., having thoughts about emotions). For instance, let's take another look at our Cast of Characters near the front of this book. I'll name the emotions I think they're having. Right now:

- Troy is happy.
- James is depressed.
- Lexi is secretly smug.
- Roscoe is grumpy but hiding it well.

Figure out emotional labels like these in real-life situations and you can win the prize every time. Meanwhile, back at the ranch, you can name all the blue-ribbon cows in your personal collection.

Emotional Intelligence for an Empath

Here's how to use Emotional Intelligence on Emotions Day — and whenever else you wish to turn off unskilled empath merges. Remember that *feeling* other people's feelings is optional. Instead you can substitute Emotional Intelligence.

As a born empath, you're fully capable of doing a Skilled Empath Merge, as appropriate (Once you've learned how. We'll get there!) But that's powerful, not something to do casually whenever some random human being crosses your path.

In most cases, you'll choose NOT to do a Skilled Empath Merge. What then? Rather than feeling other people's emotions directly, you can merely recognize them. As you get used to this far less exhausting way of being with other people, you may find it helpful to *name* their different emotions inwardly. (Not doing this forever, more like training wheels until you can balance on your skilled empath's two-wheeler.)

Naming allows you to make contact with emotions in a way that will show in your face, voice, and behavior. So you can act appropriately, yet you'll be spared what it's like to emotionally roller-coast your way through a conversation. Feeling other people's feelings along with them — why bother to do that ever again? Having a simple conversation is plenty.

Emotional Intelligence: So Surfacey, So Simple

Fear not, using Emotional Intelligence on other people, Brave Explorer. Try it, just for today. Also use Emotional Intelligence on yourself occasionally: Notice a strong mood. Name it. Move on.

Locating emotions, right on the surface, can protect you from reflexively diving into your deepest feelings. You'll find it easier to keep your empath gift(s) turned OFF. Beyond, that superficial bit of self-recognition can make an empath less likely to project feelings onto others.

Some of you empaths already may find it super easy to name your own emotions. But others may find it challenging (so far). You may even find, to your horror, that you seem to have no emotions whatsoever. Well, our next technique can help with that.

Emotional GPS

Being human, at any given time, you always have at least one emotion. And you were born with a Global Positioning System (GPS) for finding simple words to locate the name.

To prepare for this technique, have pen and paper handy.

Also, prevent interruptions. Emotional GPS won't take you long, and you have every right to claim those five minutes.

In order to locate a name for whatever you're feeling, right here and now:

1. Close your eyes.
2. Take a deep breath.
3. Notice which emotion(s) you have.
4. If names aren't obvious, ask inside for some words. Emotions have names, and you know those names. Asking will help you to make contact with the appropriate name, no effort needed.
5. Optional: If you feel the least bit stuck, don't concentrate or struggle. Take two slow, deep breaths; then repeat Steps 3-4.
6. Open your eyes just long enough to write down whatever names you get.
7. Inside, say something like, "Good job! And now this technique is done."
8. Open your eyes.

Look over what you just wrote. Soon you'll find it super-easy to name your emotions. It can be fun.

However, some of you Brave Explorers may not notice any emotions at all. (Not yet.) Or you may even call some emotions words about something else, like theories or your personal energies.

Then it's time to do some problem solving. Don't let any problems discourage you, because you definitely have what it takes to find and name your emotions.

Let the Q&A about Emotions Begin

For decades, I have worked with clients and students. Often I have asked them to name what they are feeling emotionally. Most of them don't do this very well, not at first. But after a little problem solving, they find it easy. That's why I'm so sure all of you can develop that naming skill and then use it. Easily.

Let's do problem solving now in the form of fictional Q&A conversations with empaths who find it hard to name their emotions. Thus far, none of the following questioners has made contact with an emotion and managed to name it. Yet they're oh-so-close.

Mostly problems arise when people don't aim their consciousness in the right direction for finding an emotion. Soon as you read the following question, can you spot what's wrong?

MEG'S Question

Q. In my childhood I used to have the most wonderful time choosing how I would wish upon a star. That's an emotion, isn't it?

A. That's an idea *from* your intellect, an idea *about* an emotion — which is not the same thing as an actual emotion.

What shows me that your words have come from your intellect? You were describing a memory, not an experience in the here and now.

Intellect is fine, and you certainly don't have to destroy your intellect in order to make contact with your emotions. Your goal is to use all the different categories within yourself: Mind, body, spirit, intellect, soul, emotions, environment. Only the goal is also to use each category for what it does best, not as a substitute for another type of inner perception.

Most of these categories work only in present time: Emotions, mind, body, soul and environment. Only intellect and spirit can move a person through space and time.

"In my childhood I used to" is, therefore, a tipoff that you have shifted to intellect. Hold on, Intellect Day is not today!

Take it easy, Meg. Close your eyes. Go inside and explore the feeling connected to "I used to have the most wonderful time making a wish upon a star." Poke around. You're sure to find at least one emotion. It might be:

- Wistful
- Nostalgic
- Tragic
- Hopeful

Feel it, even a little. And then soon you can name it. Score that as a triumph for Emotions Day.

JAMES' Question

Q. *There's some vague, personal thing in there. But I don't know what it is, nor do I particularly want to know. Yuck. Can I just skip this assignment?*

A. Aw, emotions can't hurt you. Not with a simple exercise like this. Sometimes emotions are vague, sometimes not. Yet every one counts. If you see a cow in the fog, it's still a cow, not a barn.

How can I persuade you that it's safe to name your emotions? Must you purchase a tree-shaped room deodorizer for distracting yourself, maybe hold it near your nose for the rest of Emotions Day?

Come on, James. Think harmless, contented cows. Then close your eyes and go inside to find some emotions. If you're not sure what to name that feeling inside you, hang around it and ask. Eventually you'll find something that you can name.

HANNAH'S Question

Q. *In my heart chakra there's a pointy place that feels very sharp. Am I good at this naming emotions or what?*

A. Nice try. Soon as you start noticing chakras, you're experiencing from the spirit category of yourself. Energy flows, colors, lights — it's all very interesting. But energy is not the same as emotion.

Point your consciousness differently, that's all. For today, be especially interested in human emotions. Yours.

JOCELYN'S Question

Q. *My guides tell me that I am feeling angry. Do I get extra points for having the knowledge come from a higher source?*

A. Consulting spirit guides is not recommended, now that we're living in The Age of Awakening. This began on December 21, 2012. You can learn about what changed and why I don't recommend talking with guides any longer, thanks to a different book, "The New Strong."

For now, please take my word for it, Jocelyn. Guides will not help you to gain Empath Empowerment. So thank your guides for their service and ask them to go back to working in the background to help you. They'll do that just fine; it's in their original job description.

Meanwhile, back at you. And developing empath skills. Developing them as a human being. You, that human person, are in charge here. That's important because, frankly, you are the one who suffers when STUFF from other people comes into your aura. And only you, not your guides, can help you develop the skill set of Empath Empowerment.

Please, do our "Emotional GPS" technique again. Make direct contact, on your own, with emotions. Name 'em. Then write them down. And maybe congratulate yourself!

ZACHARY'S Question

Q. *What if I don't know what to call these emotions? Isn't it enough to feel them without bothering to find names?*

A. Feeling directly is good. But if you want to develop skill as an empath, you'll definitely need to use your words. Once you get into your emotions, you can find plenty of names for them. Just ask, as in our "Emotional GPS" technique.

It's like being back at the ranch, naming pet cattle. At first, you might feel shy. You're tempted to call them all "Rover." But soon you'll find all the names you need. For starters, here are some useful names for basic human emotions:

- Happy
- Sad
- Scared
- Angry

Stampede

Fear not the stampede. If you were really tending a herd of animals that weighed as much as 1,000 pounds each, and they got themselves the notion of running together in some random fashion, this could be severely challenging for you, the cowboy.

But our cows here are only a cute analogy.

So what do I mean when I bring up the possibility of a stampede?

Say that you're hanging out with your buddies Jocelyn, Troy. and Hannah. Today being Emotions Day, your plan is to "use" your emotions as a way to bring awareness away from others and back to yourself. But what if you really don't want to? What if, inside, you're feeling resistance like this?

No, not there. Definitely not, I don't want to. Grrr.

How horrible that I would ever have done this zany experiment and try these stoooopid techniques, for which I would say that I feel the utmost contempt, except that possibly "contempt" might be considered an emotion, and I am not, repeat NOT, going to notice any emotions.

Why? Because they make me so annoyed and frustrated, that's why.

Notice some emotional words there? Perchance an emotional undertone?

Any strong disinclination to investigate your own emotions is suspect. Frankly, what I suspect is this: If only you close your eyes, take a deep breath and gently pay attention, within two seconds you'll find at least one emotion. And you can give it a name.

It may be one emotion or many, stampeding around. Or it could just be one emotion: *Conrad, The Mighty 10-Ton Bull of Fear.*

Remember this saying: "The only thing we have to fear is fear itself."

If you're scared of emotions, that's called "feeling scared." If you're angry about having too many emotions or having too few, either way, that's called "feeling angry." No emotion can kill you. That would be called "death." And death is not an emotion.

Your Assignment for Day 10

Live a little today. Live on the wild side. Use Emotional GPS whenever you need to. Do it especially if another person is having strong emotions and you're tempted to join in.

Otherwise you'd be bringing on extra unskilled empath merges, which have dubious value for helping *anyone.*

What about you empaths with gifts that don't involve emotion? You can do Emotion Day too, you know. Especially important since you may have the habit of experiencing other people's emotions indirectly.

What do I mean by "indirectly"?

For instance, let's say that Troy is feeling very upset. If you have Physical Oneness, you might shift into an experience of what that intense emotion does in his body. And, because this is a "oneness" gift, rather than an "intuition" gift, the tension would be felt within your own body as if it really belonged to you.

If you slipped up in this way, you might think that Troy's physical tension was your problem. And soon it would be. (Wakeup Call is the remedy for such problems, remember?)

Whatever your gift(s) as an empath, when someone else's emotions are very intense, you can be pulled into unskilled Empath Merges, taking on STUFF galore.

Don't go there. Make the very slight, subtle shift of consciousness required to turn your gift(s) OFF.

Remember, you don't have to struggle to do this. Nor need you improvise techniques for "coping" or "boundaries" or self-protection. Techniques you're learning with our 30-Day Plan will protect you just fine, and with considerable finesse.

Today, for instance, you're specializing in turning your empath gift(s) OFF by experimenting with Emotions Day. At least three times today, consciously pay attention to what you are feeling here and now. This will prevent unskilled empath merges. Besides, it's fun to live among those crazy cows called "emotions."

DAY 11

Spiritual Awareness Day

God can help you to become a skilled empath. That would be your version of God, of course. He or She might be part of a religion that brings you inspiration, comfort, a sense of connection to something bigger than yourself.

But what if organized religion doesn't appeal? You might prefer what I call "disorganized religion." Whatever! Something about life is sacred to you, something deeper than people, places and random events. Today you get to enjoy That as a way to help you to activate a category of your human self, useful for stopping those unskilled empath merges.

Your spiritual team could have a name like this:

- Me, a good Catholic (or Evangelical Christian, or upstanding Buddhist, or faithful Muslim, or devoted Hindu, or nice Jewish girl from New York, etc.)
- Me plus my Highest Power
- Me, who believes most in my family and wants to be strong and healthy for their sake
- Me and my spiritual search for meaning
- Me, enhanced by one super-duper angel committee

Become Just a Bit More Demanding, Please

Many empaths are in a spiritual rut. (As are many non-empaths, too, so no need to sob especially loudly.) If you're in a spiritual rut, you can move out of it. Today! Simply by acting a bit more demanding!

Think of God as a huge ocean of magical healing water. Most people approach God holding a thimble, begging and pleading to let it be filled. Well, today you are invited to approach God with a much bigger container, maybe the size of a gigantic swimming pool, and ask for that to be filled instead.

What, you think God will refuse, groaning "Aw, that's too hard"? We're talking about a spiritual resource that created this entire amazing planet and more.

Whenever you ask God to help your inner life, it's impossible to ask too much. Give yourself permission to ask big. Demand that God give you more than a thimble-sized blessing.

Ask for huge amounts of self-love, self-confidence, spiritual awakening, clarity, personal power. Or choose anything else that will strengthen you.

Which Favors, When?

Here's another way that you can make life better during Spiritual Awareness Day (and beyond). Starting today, if you find somebody else in trouble, quit acting as if you are the only possible resource. Sadly, unskilled empaths can misuse their compassion by choosing thoughts like these:

- Gee, I wish I could help you feel better.
- I really feel for you.
- If only there were something that I, personally, could do to take away your suffering.
- If only I could do even more.
- How I wish I could take away that terrible pain/fear/anger/suffering.

Have you been trying to help others in ways like this? 'Fess up. Then, please, cut it out.

Your heart has been in the right place, but — if I may be frank — your technique stinks.

Any of the previous requests will cause you to do a quick, or not-so-quick, unskilled empath merge with the troubled person. You'll do this repeatedly. (Though probably not consciously.) Consequently you'll pick up Imported STUFF from his/her aura and keep it hanging around in your own personal aura for an indefinite amount of time.

Sweet? Yes. Smart? No, not when you can use the "Take It" technique instead.

Next time you're in a situation where somebody needs help, first, consider if there is something practical you can do on the level of objective reality, like take out the garbage or send a condolence card. Decide if you really, truly are willing to do this.

Don't volunteer just because another person has a need. And before you volunteer to do anything bigger than sending a card, ask the other person if he or she even wants you to do it, such as, "Would you like me to take out the garbage?"

Volunteering to help with *objective-reality* actions? That's just common courtesy to help anyone, whether you're an empath or not. That said, let's get back to the topic of *subjective* volunteering, that old, familiar kind of volunteering so favored by unskilled empaths. Here's a simple alternative.

Take It

What if you happen to notice that somebody else is suffering? Suppose that you'd like to help that person spiritually and/or energetically.

Must you continue to use the old "I'll take it" method of unskilled empath-dom? Instead you could substitute this method. Probably you'll help that person more effectively.

And speaking of substituting, in the following technique I'll use the name "X" to represent the person you wish to help.

When doing the technique that follows, substitute that name if you know it. Otherwise use a simple description like "that man I just saw on the street."

1. Choose a personal form of God to help you when doing Take It on this particular occasion. For instance you could choose God or, alternatively, a Divine Being in a body — like Jesus, Buddha, Kwan Yin, Krishna, Archangel Michael, Archangel Gabriel or Athena.
2. Say the name once. Notice, I didn't just ask you to necessarily "believe in," "worship," "visualize," etc. None of this is necessary for this technique to work properly. Soon as you can do this appropriately, say that name once. Out loud. Quality. (No screaming required.)
3. Quick as thought, that Divine Being will show up. No kidding. This statement isn't based just on my personal experience but from teaching this super-easy technique to students in many parts of the world. The Divine Being you have requested will instantly appear in His or Her body of super-high-vibrational light. Incidentally, He or She will definitely NOT demand to see your membership card for any particular religious organization.
4. Say a sentence like this: "Please help X."
5. Really, that's quite specific enough. Avoid outlining what you believe is the important spiritual outcome. Quite possibly, God might know better than you.
6. Although Divine Beings are omniscient, their help does not activate automatically. It's important that we humans co-create, as you've just done. (To learn more, explore my Spiritually Sparkling® online workshops.)
7. Finally, to finish the Divine co-creation you just set in motion clean up. Say out loud, "Divine Being, please cut all astral ties between me and X. Then fill both of us with Divine love, light, and power."

Yes, Take It is just that simple.

Powerful, nonetheless. Based on research I've done with students and clients worldwide, I'm convinced that Take It works every time. The Divine Being will remove as much as is possible to remove, which equals at least as much as you, personally, would have removed temporarily through an unskilled empath merge.

Only, not meaning to insult you, fact is: God does this kind of job better.

Hey, It Even Works for Zachary

Here's an example of applying the Take It technique. Say that you're visiting with your pal Zachary when suddenly you notice that he's upset about something. Yes, the guy's definitely sad.

By now you own the "Take It" technique. So your best way of helping is NOT to share Zachary 's sadness. You don't have to "feel for him" since he's already doing a perfectly fine job of being in contact with his own misery.

Instead, talk to Zachie. Find out more about what's going on with him. Following that, take a break. Move out of earshot. Then use those seven steps you just learned.

Easy-peasy. And now you can go back to being a good friend to Zach. But now you're acting like a good friend who also happens to be The Most Important Person in the Room!

You see, Divine Beings have a different kind of body from us humans. They can help beautifully. And they help with no strings attached. Only they won't usually help without an invitation from someone in human form.

Look, I didn't make those rules. That's just how it is here at Earth School.

Another rule for doing Take It is this: Although asking for help is perfectly fine, you don't have the right to micromanage Divine

Beings. Take It is simple. Purposely simple. Spiritually it would be tacky to demand something like this:

Take away Zachary's pain by giving him $4 million right now. Then would you please give him the guts to finally quit that job he hates so much? While you're at it, fix his tendency to spoil his kids rotten, because that isn't making his life any easier either. Euww, those bratty kids are so annoying!

To summarize, Take It works just fine, provided that you co-create rather than try to boss around. You're becoming The Most Important Person in The Room, not The Most Important Person in The Universe.

Your Assignment for Day 11

Today's assignment is simple.

1. Include this in your day: three 2-minute periods where you sit, close your eyes, and inwardly make contact with the Divine Being of your choice.
2. Experiment at least once with the "Take It" technique
3. Of course, you'll continue with Be Deep as inspired.

DAY 12

Soul Day

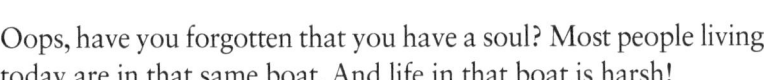

Oops, have you forgotten that you have a soul? Most people living today are in that same boat. And life in that boat is harsh!

Before explaining what you can do to improve things, I had better define what I mean by "soul" in the first place.

Soul is different from spirit, although many people mix these terms up. Both begin as a divinely designed chunk of what makes you YOU.

This quirky one-of-a-kind quality has been you since you first were created. The You-ness makes you at least as unique as a snowflake. And since you're not a snowflake but a big-deal Divine creation, that You-ness lasts for longer than the time it takes to thaw. Your individuality is eternal.

For this particular lifetime, your You-ness expresses in two different ways.

Your Spirit

Your spirit longs to connect back to source. This makes you like E.T. in the Spielberg movie, constantly trying to return back to the mother ship. Okay, maybe you don't walk around whimpering "E.T. phone home."

Nonetheless, ever since childhood, you have been developing your own methods to phone home, like these:

- ∼ Gazing at a beautiful sunset
- ∼ Falling in love

- Wishing on a star, a birthday cake, a dandelion
- Eating chocolate
- And, probably, all those things that you did yesterday for Spiritual Awareness Day

When the search for spiritual connection works right, it brings great relief. You want that moment to last forever.

How spiritual it is, desiring to end the homesickness! Also very much related to your spirit: How you may yearn to know, beyond the shadow of a doubt, that you are eternally one with God.

Your Soul

By contrast, your soul is how You-ness expresses in this particular human incarnation. Some choices make you feel great, others don't. For instance you have:

1. **Favorite foods (a.k.a. soul food — and for you it doesn't have to be fried chicken and collards)**
2. **Favorite music (a.k.a. soul music — which, for you, could be polkas, waltzes, whatevers)**
3. **Favorite ways to be affectionate (e.g., soul kiss — enough said)**

Living with soul ought to be the most natural thing in the world. Actually, it was… when you were about two years old. But then you learned manners.

Sigh! For better or worse, you also learned how to understand words like "should."

Nothing can kill your soul. But if anything came close, surely it would be the word "should."

Don't get me wrong. Doing one's duty is necessary. It makes the world go around (at least as much as love does). But consider this: On any given day, how many things do you choose merely because you're supposed to?

Joyless, dutiful, responsible, "adult" behavior. Yecch!

Most adults don't spend even one hour a day doing what they need and want as human beings.

Take exercise, for example. Do you work out regularly? If so, perhaps you dutifully run on some treadmill. Or do you, instead, pursue a form of exercise that makes you go "Yabba dabba doo"? (Substitute words from your personal inner language of bliss. It's one of those very private, soulful things about you.)

Maybe your soul would prefer for you to dance naked around the house.

Lexi would rather practice picking up marbles between her toes.

Zachary would rather stomp around the bedroom, splashing himself with aftershave while he practices grunting.

Have you asked your soul lately which form of exercise would be *fun*? Or do you resign yourself, as most adults do, slapping a big, bored smile on your face as you "get with the (virtuous-seeming) program"?

Your Soul Deserves Better

Soul Thrill® Aura Research has become one of my specialties as the founder of RES. Based on researching thousands of auras, I've found that 299 out of 300 people living today aren't living with soul at all. Anyone can, however. You, for instance.

All it takes is spending one hour each day, doing any combo of things that thrill your soul. More than one hour won't hurt. It's just not required.

Really, all you need is that one daily hour of soul thrill, 10 minutes here plus 5 minutes there, etc.

Consider it a soul-level vitamin. You've got a minimum daily requirement. Meet that and you'll find life considerably more enjoyable.

Sound good? Know that you can get it.

Start today. Become a person who lives with soul thrill. Spend an hour a day... doing what delights you.

Besides making your life more fulfilling, living with soul will help you to become a skilled empath.

Why would that be? For one reason, The Most Important Person in The Room does not spend most waking hours feeling like a galley slave.

Besides that, you're more likely to fully enjoy yourself in the moment. Consequently, you'll avoid feeling guilty about focusing on yourself.

Yes, I'm boldly suggesting that one under-reported cause of guilt is simply not having enough fun.

When you're having a really good time, you've got some serious momentum going, right? Guilt can precede or follow a really good time, not happen during. While really enjoying yourself, you're far too busy having fun... to doubt yourself.

And. trust me, you don't have to quit your job to express your soul. Be sneaky about it, if you must, by using the following technique.

Take a Soul Break

At work, give yourself a 10-second soul break. Occasionally. For instance, do one of the following.

- Look around the room until you find a color that really appeals to you. Close your eyes and imagine that a paint bucket filled with that color is being poured over your head. Let the energy of that color be absorbed wherever your body needs it most.
- Whistle.
- Fill a coffee cup with water, bend upside down, and drink from the far-away edge.
- Daydream about a favorite vacation, past or future.

- ∽ Imagine that you have been given five million dollars. Think about one thing FOR YOURSELF that you would do with the money.
- ∽ Take a big, full-bodied stretch. And, while you're doing this, add a good, solid yawn — or a fake yawn, if necessary. (In this context, fake yawns work fine.)

Once you start making contact with the category of yourself called "Soul," you'll generate loads of soulful things you can do. At dinner, for instance, eat something really delicious, not merely convenient or virtuous.

If that's not possible, sit somewhere secluded and eat like a kid. Honestly, when was the last time you played with your food? Do you have any idea what you're missing?

Here's another example of soulful lifestyle: Tonight, when you have spare time, don't meekly sit in front of the TV or do the same-old Internet-schtick. Choose something else, something non-virtual and human, something that appeals to you.

Your Assignment for Day 12

Wherever you go during your waking hours today, whoever is with you, I invite you to somehow make today a golden day, a gusto kind of day. As much as possible, do what makes you happy.

Just don't get yourself fired or arrested.

And when you're with other people today, please, please, oh pretty please:

1. Continue to make yourself The Most Important Person in The Room.
2. Be Deep occasionally.
3. Once or twice today, give yourself a Wakeup Call.

DAY 13

Bingo

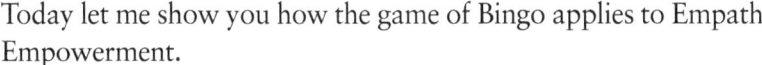

Today let me show you how the game of Bingo applies to Empath Empowerment.

A Bingo card contains five categories, famously known as B.I.N.G. and O. Your inner self contains more than five categories because you are way more exciting than a typical Bingo card.

Which are your inner categories? Mind. Body. Spirit. Intellect. Soul. Emotions. and Environment.

None of these matters most. I put them in this particular order just because I like the acronym: **MBS. I SEE!**

In Bingo, there's a Caller who randomly draws one token at a time. It's numbered within a category, like B12 or N43. After a token is called, you check your scorecard to see if your card matches up.

Maybe you'll use a colorful ink dauber to keep track as you go. Accumulate five big, red blobs in a row and you can be the one who stands up screaming with total abandon, "Me, me, I win. Bingo!"

In the empath's game I call "Inner Bingo," who gets to be The Caller? You, nobody else.

Besides that, you get to be The Player.

In addition, have you guessed? You just might become The Lucky Winner.

Inner Bingo

For this self-awareness technique, don't draw out tokens. Stop the action in the scene where you are right now. Lightly, quickly, analyze which of your inner categories has been active. Add percentages if you wish.

Instead of B.I.N.G. and O., your categories are Mind, Body, Spirit, Intellect, Soul, Emotions and Environment. Recognizing **MBS. I see!** can help you to win at the game of life.

Here are examples of how you might win at Inner Bingo.

- You're texting Hannah, laughing your head off at her amazing wit and wisdom: Intellect 80%, Emotions 20%
- You're at work, taking a mental health break, contemplating how you might like your job more: Spirit 80%, Soul 10%, Intellect 10%
- Back home, you're cleaning up the kitchen. Darn it, you are bored like crazy. Still, the chore must be done: Mind 100%

However you score, you win by virtue of playing. Unlike the traditional version of Bingo, there's no wasting time with a missed round, where somebody else gets to score and you don't.

Whatever you find when you check inside, you will always find at least one active category. So you win.

So long as you play this game quick & sloppy.

Yes, Quick & Sloppy

No precision needed. All you're after here is a quick act of self-recognition. Doing that self-recognition means something important: You're positioning consciousness at yourself, rather than other people.

And this silly game can become as effortless and shallow as playing Bingo. How complicated is it to figure out, "Do I have B9?"

Skill and comfort at paying attention to yourself: This turns you into The Most Important Person in The Room.

Whenever you shift attention from somebody else to yourself, what else happens? Automatically your empath gift(s) turn OFF. So you stop taking on other people's STUFF. Re-set! And such a win for you!

Inner Bingo is a here-and-now way to remind yourself of the richness and potential variety of your inner life.

Your Categories for Inner Bingo

In the past, you've surely heard the expression "mind-body-spirit." How limiting! During our 30-Day Plan, you've had personal experience with Mind Day, Intellect Day, etc. So you know that you have more to you than those three puny M.B.S. categories. Let's summarize all seven exciting basics of Inner Bingo, your categories of **MBS I see!**

Bingo 1. Mind

Your simplest inner functioning, mind is experienced as thoughts. Also, your mind links subjective and objective experience.

Bingo 2. Body

Awareness of your physical body could be anything from head to toes, front to back, left to right. You might feel that body at skin-level, in muscles, etc.

Just keep this way of paying attention… quick and shallow. If you start noticing sensations in your liver or tendons, you're going in to deep. Keep. It. Simple. Smarties.

Bingo 3. Spirit

Noticing energy, auras, movement, colors or silence — spirit shows up as subtle experiences of any kind within regular reality; like, closing your eyes, you might feel as though twirling around.

Can you be feeling things like this even though, physically, you're just sitting still. Sure. And doesn't that make sense? When such things happen, you're not hallucinating, simply having a perception from the spirit category… about yourself. Technique Time!

Bingo 4. Intellect

Complex, sophisticated inner functioning, experienced as thoughts — that's your intellect. As you've learned, this differs from the simpler quality of thoughts from the mind category. By contrast, your intellect includes abilities like thoughts about thoughts, creativity, discernment, learning new concepts and multi-tasking.

Bingo 5. Soul

You have very personal desires, likes and dislikes, and a keen sense of your own truth. This counts. It even counts as a category. Soul is your most intense and personal experience of yourself as a human being.

Bingo 6. Emotions

Feelings in this category are expressed with words like happy, sad, scared, angry. A beginner might confuse emotions with other inner experiences, like "Lots of energy" (Spirit) or "Achy" (Body).

How to move from words like these to words that will be more informative about emotions? Ask yourself a question like, "When I am achy right now, how does that make me feel emotionally?"

Bingo 7. Environment

Whether with others or alone, indoors or outdoors, here and now, you always have a way of being yourself in the environment.

It's your social self. The particular version of yourself changes according to the situation, so you act one way with your mother, another with your brother, yet another with your boss at work.

This social version of yourself, here and now, is "Your personal way of being in the environment right now" or ENVIRONMENT for short.

Which components of your mind-body-spirit-intellect-soul-emotions-environment are you using when? Today's technique helps you pay attention. You're not changing a thing, simply noticing.

Inner Bingo need not be more complicated than checking a physical Bingo card. After all, you're well prepared. Earlier assignments from our 30-Day Plan have given you exceptional familiarity with five of your categories.

Only one remains to be explored, Environment. So….

Hello, Environment!

"Environment" simply means your social setting. Especially *who you are*, in that particular social setting. Back when you were an unskilled empath you may have felt reluctant to experience yourself in different social settings. Remember what that was like, 13 days ago?

Often you felt like a chameleon. Typically, you were The Least Important Person in The Room, someone invisible. Other people's versions of Environment might have seemed to outweigh yours. My, how you have changed, already. And not even halfway through this Empath Empowerment Program!

As you become even more skilled as an empath, you'll discover fascinating nuances in how you're yourself when in one social Environment or another. Have you experienced any of the following changes? (If not yet, expect to start noticing soon. Just keep on doing your daily assignments.)

1. Dressing for the Occasion

We empaths can fall into some pretty self-dismissive habits regarding our clothing. Maybe dressing up as if competing in a contest, aiming to impress others, constantly comparing. Or maybe dressing down to "be comfortable" — totally ignoring how you appear to others. The art of dressing as a social activity can torment an unskilled empath in so many ways. Only now it's becoming a game you can win.

UNSKILLED EMPATH: When other people look at how I'm dressed, I see how they react to me. And that's the main thing I notice.

SKILLED EMPATH: I notice how I'm dressed, and it pleases me.

2. Random Volunteering

Helping others can be beautiful, when you consciously choose to volunteer. But volunteering as a way of life? Or random volunteering, simply because somebody else happens to be in the room with you? That stinks.

UNSKILLED EMPATH: When someone's around me, like Zachary, I feels uncomfortable. Both physically and emotionally! I can't help but notice and wish I could help. (Resulting immediately in an unskilled empath merge.)

SKILLED EMPATH: When with Zachary, even if he's suffering, my first loyalty is to myself. Not to him. Sometimes I might decide to use the "Take It" technique on him, but I never volunteer to such an extent that I lose the main focus of my life, which is me. Speaking of which….

3. Positioning Attention

Usually it's automatic, how you position attention. Unfortunately, we empaths often have the habit of automatically paying attention to everyone else in the room. Not one's own sweet self! Well, that sure can change.

UNSKILLED EMPATH: When other people, like Zachary, are around, I can't stay completely focused on what I'm doing. Instead, I pay a lot of attention to what Zachary needs, and what he thinks of me.

Skilled Empath: I can stay focused on whatever I'm doing, regardless of reactions from Zachary. Basically, I have my own way of doing whatever I'm doing in this particular social situation. That's plenty. Because I'm living my life directly. No longer through the eyes of other people.

4. Staying Interested in Yourself

Does it make you selfish, paying attention to yourself? Definitely not! Especially when you're a skilled empath. Non-empaths automatically treat themselves as The Most Important Person in the Room. And it's perfectly fine for you to do it too.

Unskilled Empath: When with other people, like Zachary, I'm very aware of how I could help him, what's going on with him, etc. All that information streams through me, drowning out my sense of self.

Skilled Empath: When with other people, even someone as fascinating as Zachary, that doesn't keep me from having my own sense of self, complete with personal goals and desires. Zachary may come or go, but this is my life. I come first.

5. Sense of Self

Look, you wouldn't purposely give other people the power to tell you who you are, right? Sadly, many an unskilled empath does that constantly. (At least, until becoming a skilled empath.)

Unskilled Empath: I tend to become who other people think I am. Talk that way. Adopt body language to match other people's expectations. Ick!

Skilled Empath: I stay myself, doing what I do, feeling as I feel, unapologetically saying and doing things in my own way.

Brave Explorer, putting yourself first can be fun. Not wicked fun, human fun. Inner Bingo helps you to sort out which kind of fun you are having. **MBS. I see!**

6. Sexual Self-Confidence

Actually, you could interpret all you've just read about Environment for a Skilled Empath… in terms of sex. In any environment where there's a chance for sex, skilled empaths will appear sexier than unskilled empaths. We're simply more fully present.

UNSKILLED EMPATH: I tend to feel only as sexy as other people think I am.

SKILLED EMPATH: I'm naturally confident sexually, doing what I do, feeling as I feel, unapologetically being who I am.

Your Assignment for Day 13

Play Inner Bingo at least five times. At random intervals, pause inwardly, close your eyes and notice:

- Among your seven categories, which ones are most active right now, mind, body, spirit, intellect, soul, emotions or environment?
- Approximate the percentage for each. Make note on a pad of paper, by texting yourself, wherever.

No need to be precise or double-check the math to be sure that your score adds up to a perfect 100%. Nor does this technique require that you change a thing. You're simply learning about yourself, specifically your habits for using mind-body-spirit-intellect-soul-emotions-environment.

Just for fun, guess right now: What will Inner Bingo show you today? Do you think that you will use the same category of self, over and over? During a full set of waking hours, might you use 3 or 5 or all 7?

Find out, because you might be pleasantly surprised. Regardless, the very act of playing Inner Bingo will strengthen you as an empath.

DAY 14

Advanced Bingo

Yesterday you started playing Inner Bingo, catching yourself at random moments, then noticing which categories of self were most active. Did you find yourself favoring one or two categories out of habit (like Intellect, Spirit, or Environment)? Then let's help you become more resourceful as a person by adding the technique I call "Advanced Bingo."

Perhaps you don't need that kind of help. Maybe yesterday's assignment revealed that you're already using your full set of categories. Even then, the skill you learn today can help you, because it's so useful for helping you deal with people when they're suffering.

Suppose that your plans for today involve spending time with your friend Jocelyn, and she happens to be very depressed. If you engage with her by living mainly from the Emotions category, that could spell trouble. Instead, for part of your visit, use Advanced Bingo to move into a different part of yourself, such as Mind, Soul or Body. Just one quick shift does it.

Not only will you feel better. You'll find it far easier to keep your empath gift(s) nicely turned OFF.

Similarly, you could be living mostly from Body Awareness but you decide to change that while hanging out with Roscoe. How come? He's such a fierce hypochondriac.

Or how about dealing with Hannah? Mostly she's a fabulous friend but her intellect is on overdrive. If you follow her lead and shift into living mostly from Intellect, that could lead to a headache (figuratively or even literally).

Keep This Simple. You Can.

For Advanced Bingo to work, you don't have to assess other people the way I just did. You don't need to figure out how they emphasize one category of life or another.

Remember, the skill set for Empath Empowerment is supposed to be effective but easy. Let simple discomfort be your cue: "What, I'm starting to feel uncomfortable hanging out with Roscoe? Time to do Advanced Bingo!"

Soon as you start feeling drained by another person, do our latest technique.

Advanced Bingo

To play Advanced Bingo, reach inside the token tumbler of yourself (one quick thought does it) and pull out N37. I mean Body awareness, Mind awareness or some other personal kind of awareness that is different from the category you have been using before.

Give just the tiniest inner nudge to your inner self. Your consciousness will do the rest.

Brave Explorers, it's important to understand how easy Advanced Bingo can be. Our 30-Day Plan has familiarized you with all the categories of yourself. More strongly than before, you "own" each of them. It's your **MBS. I see!** So you can use this however you wish.

As for the amount of effort necessary for our new technique, it's ridiculously teensy. Has this ever happened to you? Playing regular Bingo, you need just one particular token pulled so that you can win. Inside you're yelling, pushing hard, "Pick N37, N37. I must have N37."

Only the tiniest fraction of that effort is needed to play Advanced Bingo. And win! Soon as you choose Body rather than Mind or Intellect, etc., bam, you've got it! Just one quick thought. Inwardly, you can be all body, all whatever, all the time... at least for the next few minutes.

Say that you choose to bring awareness to the Body category. Suddenly you will start noticing all sorts of interesting things about your left foot, your nasal passages, whatever seems new and fascinating in the world of My Personal Body Sensations. A fine show indeed!

Being there for Jocelyn

Just because Advanced Bingo is easy, don't underestimate its power to help you as an empath. In this example, your friend Jocelyn is upset over something and you're being there for her, as any good friend would. Did you ever consider the meaning of that common expression, "Being there for someone"? That can be done very suavely right on the surface of life.

What is required for "being there," showing support to a friend like Jocelyn? Physically be present. Listen to her words. Show a sympathetic attitude.

Guess what? This is all non-empaths do, "being there" for someone. Only empaths are wacky enough to routinely interpret "Being there for her" like this:

- Unconsciously, I will merge with Jocelyn's aura 30 super-quick times in 10 minutes, lifting STUFF from her aura and depositing it into mine.
- Consciously I will push myself to become very, very deeply involved.
- I will give and give, through unskilled empath merges. Giving as much to Jocelyn as possible… until her smile tells me she's satisfied.
- At the end of the hour, I will charge her the standard rate for psychiatric services.
- Just kidding about that last part.

Back to you now, as a skilled empath. Thanks to Advanced Bingo, you can act just like any non-empath, "being there" for Jocelyn by outwardly going through the motions. Human-type suppport. Don't knock it!

While doing this, thanks to Advanced Bingo, you will stay free of Jocelyn's STUFF. Thus, you can act like a good friend yet remain The Most Important Person in The Room.

Still The Most Important Person

Please repeat after me:

> ***How much must I give to anyone***
>
> ***before I'm allowed to consider myself***
>
> ***The Most Important Person in The Room?***
>
> ***Nothing!***

Hey, forget about Advanced Bingo for a moment. Forget, even about Jocelyn, fascinating though her sorrows might be. Instead imagine that somebody really important has just entered the room. Gorgeous One! Your favorite movie star. And also imagine that nothing else has changed about the place where you are now.

Don't you think you might become very aware of Gorgeous One? Like, constantly? And no matter what else is happening?

Sighting a movie star when you're out walking, dining at your neighborhood Burger King, shopping at the mall, etc.? Most otherwise "normal" people would act star struck. Immediately they would stare. And sweat. And maybe babble, "Omigod, I'm in the room with Gorgeous One. Yes, Gorgeous One, for crying out loud !!!!!!!!!!!!!!!!!!!!"

Yet meaning no insult to the fabulous Gorgeous One, why should that star be any more important to you… than you?

All I'm asking you to do today is to treat yourself like The Most Important Person in The Room, even if that room contains several Gorgeous Ones.

So let's suppose that you're in the room with Jocelyn. And you happen to spontaneously be paying attention to the Body category of your mind-body-spirit-intellect-soul-emotions-environment.

Right now, that might mean weighing and balancing physical sensations in both your earlobes. Does one happen to feel just a bit heavier right now? Hmmm, how fascinating is that?

Of course, in this example, Jocelyn has been talking away the whole time. By now she sobbing. If all that you offer her is "being there" (along with paying quality attention to yourself, Body style) are you being a good enough friend? Sure you are. Let me count the ways:

- You are keeping Jocelyn company.
- You are nodding at appropriate intervals.
- You're allowing Jocelyn to complain to her heart's content.
- As needed, you are even handing out tissues.

Besides that, you're well on your way to behaving like a skilled empath. Maybe, later in your day, you might give Jocelyn the wonderful gift of our Take It technique. Or maybe not even that.

And when your visit with Jocelyn finally ends, and you have kept your empath gift(s) nicely turned OFF the whole time, congratulations! How's this for a nice change in your life?

Leaving Jocelyn behind with a sweet "Goodbye," how about you? Enjoy the satisfaction of acting like a good friend. Plus, this time you won't feel like one of her used tissues. Instead, you will feel very much alive. And ready for your next social encounter, whether or not it includes Gorgeous One.

What, no Gorgeous One? Sigh! Well, that's life. Your life.

Your Assignment for Day 14

Just like yesterday, play Inner Bingo five random times. Only today, you'll do one thing differently. Add Advanced Bingo as needed:

What if you notice that you're favoring one category (like Emotions) again and again? Start paying attention to some different category.

And not always the same different category. But you already figured that out, didn't you, Brave Explorer?

By now you know, shifting your consciousness is easy. Whenever you wish, you can choose a different category of experience, whether mind, body, spirit, intellect, soul, emotions or your personal way of being in this environment.

Because being you means having access to all of **MBS. I see!**

One quick thought will do the job, so familiar have you become with all of your inner categories as a person. A teensy shift of consciousness will light up one of your many, many ways of living.

Play Advanced Bingo today and watch all of your life improve.

DAY 15

Say Whatever

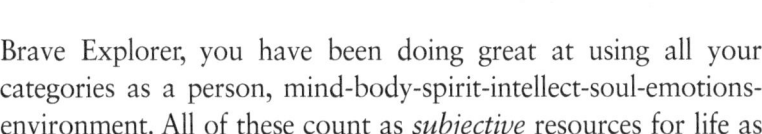

Brave Explorer, you have been doing great at using all your categories as a person, mind-body-spirit-intellect-soul-emotions-environment. All of these count as *subjective* resources for life as a skilled empath.

Today let's start to introduce some *objective* resources: Speech and action.

As an aura reader, I've noticed that many empaths carry a huge amount of clog in their Throat Chakras. Could you be at risk? Because that could come back to bite you, as it were. Compromising your empath skills. Let's solve that problem today.

Unclogging. Life's Easiest Dance

I love watching those Irish Riverdance cloggers as much as you do but, please, save the big tapping shoes for your feet. Not your neck. Actually, clogging up your Throat Chakra doesn't feel like dancing. It happens in situations like these:

- Much as you enjoy being with Meg, you resent how she treats you. Frustrated, you say nothing. Great job, except for your Throat Chakra!
- Troy talks. And talks. And talks. Politely, you hide your boredom. Unbeknownst to you, your prize for this great success at hiding is brand new STUFF entering your Throat Chakra.
- Although you disagree with Lexi while she goes on a rant, you avoid giving her feedback. So important to be polite?

So unimportant, honoring all the things you have to say? Ugh, so much clog comes into your aura, staying long after Lexi leaves the room!

- How you wish that, for once, James would quit bothering you. You *wish*. You don't say. And, therefore, you clog yourself up. Long after James has stopped trying to make you angry, new STUFF will keep doing that job just fine.
- Which kind of STUFF am I telling you about here. Not Imported STUFF. But other kinds of STUFF. To get some idea of the varieties, browse here: www.rose-rosetree.com/sessions/energy-healing/.

Why is it, people talk about "Stifling a yawn" yet never mention the deeper problem, "Stifling a Throat Chakra"?

Throat Chakra, Sure

Admittedly, most folks today wouldn't say this because they aren't sure exactly what the heck a "chakra" is. A CHAKRA is part of your aura. And your AURA is the collection of energy bodies around your physical body, full of information. All those bodies, together, count as your aura.

An aura's information is especially concentrated in chakras, places that correspond to your physical body. Think of a healthy aura as containing free-flowing energy. How can that energy flow properly when a chakra contains globs and blobs of stuck energy? (What I call "clog" or "**STUFF**.")

If you're so busy thinking of others that you swallow your words, that stuck energy doesn't just go away. One common sign of throat clog is….

Delicious Sarcasm

Yesterday I saw these words on a tee-shirt: "Sarcasm is just one of many fine services I offer."

I giggled to myself in a cool, post-postmodern sort of way. But then I went "Aha!" and designed the following technique for you (and also for me).

Sarcasm Fast

Could we possibly cut out the excess irony? Just for one day? Are you brave enough to join me in a Sarcasm Fast? Then, just for today:

1. If you hear someone else being sarcastic, sing "Thank God, I'm a Country Boy." Wait, that's not it. Think, "*Gee, that was sarcasm.*"
2. Learn from the sarcasm. Ask yourself, "Did he/she use the sarcasm *to express something* or *to keep from expressing something*?" (The latter, of course, would add more Throat Chakra clog, right?)

Even without being a fully qualified aura reader, or turning a single empath gift ON, I'll bet you can tell the difference. Most sarcasm adds to Throat Chakra clog.

If you feel the urge to say something sarcastic, don't.

Oops, if that thought comes too late, because a sarcastic remark has already left your mouth, ask yourself, "Did I use that sarcasm to express something effectively? Or was that sarcasm a signal that I just clogged up my Throat Chakra?"

Is there something not sarcastic that you could say *now*, while still in this situation? It might be as simple as, "Excuse me?" or any Throat Unclogger Sentence. (These Unclogger Sentences will be discussed soon.)

Sure, You Can Avoid Sarcasm.
And Also Break the Speech Clog Habit.

Brave Explorer, exactly how can you break the speech clog habit? One day at a time, one situation at a time.

When you feel tempted to stifle yourself, take a deep breath and ask, inwardly, "If it were safe to say whatever I wanted, what would it be?"

Here are examples of some very direct — even raw — sentences that might come to mind:

- What a nasty, ignorant thing you've just done.
- I couldn't disagree with you more, you nitwit.
- Your expression/words/behavior/body odor just hurt my feelings.

Do I recommend that you say these things? Definitely not. Nothing in this book is meant to get you fired, arrested, or divorced.

However, I am going to ask you to speak j*ust a bit* of the truth. Say enough to remove that potential Throat Chakra clog.

Throat Unclogger Sentences

What if you're worrying, "Without sarcasm, no way"?

In response, might I suggest? "Way."

All you need do is inject a Throat Unclogger Sentence into your conversation. For example:

- Excuse me, but are you aware that you just ....?
- What an interesting point of view! My opinion is different.
- What did you mean by that?

Throat Unclogger Sentences can also be helpful if you have communication problems other than sarcasm, like shyness, awkwardness in front of strangers, powerlessness, feeling left out or disconnected from a group of people, not yet knowing how to do intimacy.

Alas, those three Throat Unclogger Sentences won't completely solve all of life's problems. (Surprise me, though. If this should happen, write a Guest Post for my blog, at rose-rosetree.com. Share the miracle, because this would really be a miracle.)

Although miracles are always welcome, our goal here is humbler. For Day 15, it would be lovely if you'd master the part of Empath Empowerment that involves unnecessarily clogging up your Throat Chakra.

Guess what I have learned about Throat Unclogger Sentences, like the examples you've just learned?

> ***All it takes is one tiny non-sarcastic sentence***
> ***to avoid adding a new chunk of gunk***
> ***to your Throat Chakra.***

Remember, unclogger words spoken aloud are for your benefit. Not the other person's.

For example, suppose that you tell James, "Excuse me, but are you aware that you just insulted one of my political heroes?"

- Maybe he'll sneer at you.
- Perhaps he'll insult your political beliefs again. Only this time, speak even more rudely.
- Maybe he won't even answer. As if he has zero interest in anything you might say to interrupt his monologue.

Well, any of that would count as informative, right? Providing you with useful information about give-and-take in this relationship.

What if James does respond in a friendly way? Then you will have gently started a discussion.

And maybe even begun to improve your relationship.

Whatever the outcome, know this. For the sake of using your power, it's important to speak up for yourself.

Every empath is allowed to do that, you know. Actually, speaking up for yourself is essential for skill as an empath. Because you're learning Empath *Empowerment.*

And, like it or not, empowerment doesn't just happen to a person because you're polite. Or wish to become effective in life. Power requires saying things and doing things… in order to get more of what you want.

Will you always succeed at getting exactly what you want, just because you spoke up?

No. But I promise you. Speaking up. And doing things. That will always be informative. And then you can say more things and do more things and learn so much more. Way more than you'd learn by mostly living in your head.

Claim your empowerment, Brave Explorers!

Your Assignment for Day 15

If you know that you have absolutely no throat clog whatsoever, you get the day off. Otherwise, dare to experiment.

Just for today, Brave Explorer:

1. Avoid all sarcasm.
2. Use Throat Unclogger Sentences.
3. And, for lifelong Empath Empowerment, remember this:

   Every day from now on, in every situation,
   I can find a safe way
   to speak at least a little bit of my truth.

DAY 16

Turn Life Right Side Out

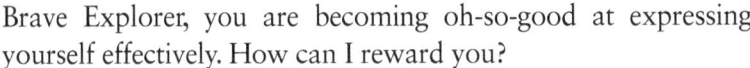

Brave Explorer, you are becoming oh-so-good at expressing yourself effectively. How can I reward you?

Allow me to present you with a brand new way to slice-and-dice reality. When was the last time you paid attention to one big, fascinating choice that everybody gets to make?

And once you understand how helpful that one choice can be for you… you'll be able to make that choice again and again.

This will be an empowering choice about POSITIONING YOUR CONSCIOUSNESS. And positioning consciousness simply means where you pay attention. At any given moment, your consciousness is positioned somewhere, but where?

We Choose One Reality at a Time

At any given moment you have a choice. Which reality will you favor, the objective version or the subjective one? Being human, you can choose only one at a time.

- **OBJECTIVE REALITY** is what happens in life, like the front section of a newspaper.
- **SUBJECTIVE REALITY** is how you feel about what happens, like the feature section of a newspaper.
- Incidentally, what about all you've learned so far about **MBS. I See!?** These are seven different ways to position your awareness subjectively.

Making the choice about where to position your consciousness can be as simple as any other slight shift of emphasis.

1. Choose.
2. Aim your consciousness.
3. Automatically you'll switch one choice on. The other goes off.

Two Very Different Realities

You can tell them apart, right, you Brave Explorer? Objective Reality and Subjective Reality are hardly identical twins.

Every human has been wired to appreciate both… and conveniently, both sides of life can always be found in the here and now. Yet often a person will get out of balance and forget that life contains both Objective and Subjective Realities. For example:

- Curmudgeonly Roscoe can act sooo **OVER-OBJECTIVE**. He jokes, "What do you mean I hurt your feelings? Show me the bruises."
- Jocelyn means well. Often, though, she acts way **OVER-SUBJECTIVE**. "I can't go to work today. I'm not in the right kind of mood."

Here's a long-overdue announcement for Roscoe and his pals: Hurt feelings are subjective but real.

And here's some news for the Jocelyns of the world: Most paying jobs aren't done on the basis of "I'm in the mood." With most jobs, you're obligated to follow an external schedule. You know, a schedule that works in Objective Reality.

Clocks are a great example of Objective Reality. And one useful thing about having a job, any job, is how it helps remind you to notice Objective Reality.

I wonder, is it possible that many empaths who think, "I hate my job" really hate Objective Reality?

Objective or Subjective?

If you have been over-subjective, let's start changing that today.

By contrast, what if you're already great at balancing Objective Reality and Subjective Reality? Then today is your golden opportunity to notice how other people position their consciousness. Skilled empaths especially need to thoroughly understand this kind of balance. So every once in a while, observe the people around you. Do they stay balanced? Or do they favor one reality over the other?

Everyone, not just empaths, can develop the habit of acting over-subjective. It's especially tempting for empaths, however, since we typically have such profound insights into others.

Sometimes we pay so much attention to what's happening with people's inner lives that we forget to notice their outer lives — objective reality. Sadly, over-subjectivity makes it impossible for us to take effective action. Until we change that? We'll miss out on empowerment.

What would be a subjective approach to problem solving? Trying to influence someone else's energy, feelings, thinking, etc. Oops! Earth School isn't set up for people to use this approach unless it is a designated session for psychotherapy, energy healing, etc.

What's a better way to get people to do more of what you want? Use objective reality skills, like speech and action.

What Is Wrong with this Story?

The following story illustrates the difference between subjective vs. objective action for problem solving. Joyce is a student of mine who has made huge progress since recounting this frustrating experience.

"On Saturday morning, Marissa came by to visit. That was fine with me. I was expecting her.

"For the first two hours, I was really enjoying myself. Then I began to wish she would go home. But Marissa stayed. And she stayed. And she stayed.

"I went through every emotion you can imagine. I felt bored, resentful, depressed, you name it. After six hours, finally, my prayers were answered. Marissa went home."

Subjective or Objective?

You do appreciate the preventable part, right? Joyce was so over-subjective, this rendered her powerless. Paying extra attention to inner agony didn't solve Joyce's problem. Nor was it necessary to drag God into her mess.

To end the unwelcome visit, Joyce needed an objective solution. All she really needed to do? Just say these magic words, "Marissa, thanks for visiting but now it is time go home."

Okay, Brave Explorer, because you got the point so well, let me reward you with an even more extreme story about over-subjective reality.

Inspiration at the Subway Crash

The following story was told triumphantly by Hiroyuki during a workshop for empaths that I gave in Tokyo.

"For years, I've had a job that I don't especially like. To get there, I take the J-R Subway line. You may know that this subway line often has problems with people committing suicide. They crash their cars into the trains. Many people are killed every year.

"Well, last week, my train had one of these fatalities. We passengers had to stand around and wait for a very long time until the subway got moving again. As I sat there waiting, I received a very important spiritual insight.

"All those people dying — that was just God's way of giving me a message. I need to get a new job. Something closer to home!"

Signs and Messages Are Subjective, Right?

Many empaths are deeply spiritual people. So we look for signs, synchronicities, messages. Well, everything that happens does NOT have to be a sign... or carry any other big subjective meaning.

A constant (subjective) search for meaning can be a way to slow down your evolution. Ironic, isn't it?

Here's the useful thing to understand, Brave Explorers. Every life event, every burp, every wilted flower, every death in your vicinity — that need not be interpreted as a cosmic sign created expressly for you.

How Many Streets Must You Clean?

Let's go for one third story of over-subjectivity. A personal tale from a certain empath coach who was born and raised in New York City. Exciting though my home town may be, let's face it. Other cities in the world are cleaner.

At one point in my development, as I walked down the street, I would take personal responsibility for cleaning up litter along my route.

"Surely I was there for a reason."

As a result, how did I walk down the street? One step. Then stop and pick up old beer cans, carrying them back to the corner trash can. Then grab a soggy paper bag with food leftovers dripping out. Dump them and then start walking all over again. Manage to get halfway down the block. Then back to that original street corner, dumping yet more garbage.

Eventually, I realized that I needed to focus on my particular journey, my destination. I didn't have to make my job in life... constantly volunteering to clean up other people's trash.

Instead, other people's trash, I realized, could be just that to me: Their trash. Not some cosmic message that I was spiritually commanded to stop and interpret subjectively; then go and fix.

Frankly, Cosmic Messages Are Over-Rated

No matter how much you wish to serve humanity, God has given you only so many hours in the day. Constantly looking for signs is a sure way to lose your focus in life and become over-subjective. Doing this, you will miss about 50% of your life (the objective part, the accomplishing part).

Instead, you can choose a spiritually meaningful life that is also balanced. You know, gaining personal empowerment.

Fixing a problem like this can be really simple. Just use your God-given ability to be objective as well as subjective. For instance, if you're taking a walk, take the walk! The following technique also can help.

Reboot Your Inner Computer

Think of yourself as a computer, an empathic one. You contain software for perfect balance of objective and subjective life. But maybe you haven't been using that program.

Here is a sentence you can say out loud to reboot your computer and switch on that program for Objective-Subjective Balance.

"I improve my Objective-Subjective Balance right now."

Why bother to say these words out loud? If you just think them, results will be limited to the subjective circuits within you. By contrast, speaking out loud produces real, live sound waves. They bounce around in the objective world.

No yelling required. Just whisper the words, if you like. But if you want this reboot to work, definitely speak the words aloud, not in your head. Effortlessly you'll improve Objective-Subjective Balance.

What do I love most about this tiny technique? How effective it is. No effort is required beyond saying that one sentence aloud.

Automatically your subconscious mind and aura will respond, and why?

Because that balancing program has been installed deep within you by the Cosmic Human Software Developer.

For extra help during Day 16, write these words on a Reminder Card:

"I improve my Objective-Subjective Balance right now."

Read it aloud to improve your Objective-Subjective Balance. You'll gain results in both spheres of life — more effectiveness in outer life plus more inner serenity.

Your Assignment for Day 16

Oh Mighty Most Important Person in The Room, is there no end to your powers? Well, shucks, there might be some, objectively.

But could you also have way more Superhero-like powers than you have been using? Effectiveness at getting things done. Things that matter in objective reality, like punctuality. Holding a job. Getting yourself quality friendships.

In short, Empath Empowerment!

Our assignment for today will help you to use your personal power. Not because of perfecting yourself subjectively -- emotionally, spiritually, energetically.

No, no! By playing the human game of accomplishing things in objective reality. Maybe your new friend.

Specifically, here's your assignment for the rest of today:

1. **Reboot Your Inner Computer at will.**

2. When you encounter a problem today, big or small, don't go all over-subjective. Describe the problem objectively out loud.
3. Then search around for something you can say or do to improve things. Something that you can do in objective reality.
4. Optional: Just for fun, notice Objective-Subjective Balance in some of the people you meet. Or watch on your favorite streaming entertainment.
5. Hopefully, everyone has a firm grasp on reality. But do some of the folks in your life cling desperately to subjective reality or instead?
6. Start thinking a bit about power. Can people get what they want just by perfecting themselves in subjective reality? Or by ignoring it? Maybe true empowerment — for any human being, not just us empaths — demands Objective-Subjective balance?

For instance, what if you're visiting your buddy James? Notice what kind of thing he talks about. Is his conversation mainly about objective reality or the subjective kind? Or might he manage to balance the two?

As for you, now that you understand today's new concepts, you're going to be able to balance better. Understanding that objective reality is not just some subjective theory. And subjective thoughts and feelings aren't, alone, going to solve problems in objective reality.

We born empaths have so much talent for subjective reality. However, that's a plus for us to use wisely. And today you're going to upgrade your Objective-Subjective Balance.

So what if your habit has been otherwise? All skilled empaths must balance the subjective and objective sides of life. Ultimately that balance is simply a form of discernment, Earth School Smarts.

DAY 17

Better Communication, Your Formula

Why isn't it smart to shoot an ant with a cannon?

Probably you don't own even one cannon, while you possess several ants. Wait, that's not the main answer. It involves math:

- Cannon way big.
- Ant way small.

Oh, those silly ant smashers! You may giggle at their foolish ways. Yet for years now, might you have been doing something comparable?

Here's a hint. Ant-with-cannon ineffectiveness is related to differences between Objective Reality and Subjective Reality. You know, your vast subjective resources are cannon-powerful. While silly, surfacey objective resources are just the right size for solving problems. Problems that inevitably occur in everyday human life.

Problems that occur whether you're a skilled empath or unskilled; only here's the big difference. Skilled empaths solve problems effectively. While unskilled empaths? Not so much. (And accumulating various kinds of STUFF? That's also a byproduct of an over-subjective approach. Like it or not.)

- Subjective Reality? Way big. Temporarily you could even get lost in there.
- Human-Type Objective Reality? Small enough for effective problem solving.

Yesterday You Began to Appreciate This

Brave Explorer, what did you notice about objective versus subjective when you did your homework yesterday?

Yes, you did that homework, surely! Gentle reminder here: To get best results from this program, take the tiny 10 minutes per day and do your homework. Since we're now on Day 17, you have less than half the book to go. Make the most of our 30-Day Plan.

Okay, assuming that you did your homework — otherwise, please go back and repeat Day 16 — did you perhaps discover any of the following to be true?

Problem Solving

To solve everyday problems, you can't depend only on subjective insights. Instead objective action is needed.

History Lesson

When facing problems, wasn't your old habit — as an unskilled empath — to go over-subjective?

Instead of taking objective action, did you spend way too much time... feeling, thinking, or analyzing? If so, how well did that work for you?

Objective-Subjective Street Smarts

Now that you've noticed which people in your life tend to go over-objective, stop and think for a minute. How do you feel about those people?

Hint: They may be precisely the folks who have disrespected you, earning your dislike in return.

Also, they may be precisely the folks who used to make you feel powerless. Hoo boy, that powerlessness is about to change. As of today!

Rebooting Your Inner Computer Is Easy

Shifting into objective mode from subjective mode wasn't hard, once you tried it, right? Just like any of the other shifts you have learned to make with our 30-Day Plan, you found an inner tipping point of consciousness, a simple choice.

When you make the shift from subjective to objective, it's as natural as wishing on a star. If anything, it's easier. Your inner self isn't light years away but here and now.

Objective Reality Can Help You Every Time

Don't blame yourself for having problems. That's life here at Earth School. Even the best relationships can include problems. And the same with meaningful work. Let's add a simple way to solve problems better. Far more practical than an unskilled empath's old standby — drift into an unskilled empath merge.

Instead, seek ways to become more effective at dealing with problem situations and problem people. And the simplest solution of all is this: Once a problem starts happening, stop emphasizing your subjective reactions. Favor objective mode instead.

Shooting an ant with a cannon won't get you precision results. Better to use an ant-sized revolver, or whatever weapon is right-sized for your battle.

A Formula for Better Communication

Here's a super-easy way to improve communication. Brave Empath, you'll find it solves many Objective-Subjective problems.
   When somebody in your life is upsetting you, pay attention to the objective circumstances. Then speak about them with a 2:1 ratio; objective, subjective, objective. Namely:
   1. When you do X...
   2. I feel Y.
   3. So please do Z.

Finally, a use for that high school algebra! Obviously, you can substitute real, meaningful words for xyz, naming specifics about the situation that bothers you. For instance:

1. Zachary, when you use your fingers instead of potato chips to scoop up my onion dip…
2. I feel grossed out. I made this dip for everyone here at the party, not just you and your fingers.
3. Would you please use potato chips from now on? Or ask me. I'll be glad to get you a spoon and plate.

Now let's fine-tune how you can use this communication formula.

Start with Objective Reality

This example of communication includes humble, everyday references to objective reality. Such as spoons and plates.

Make the Subjective Reference SURFACEY

Brave Explorer, this is the most important aspect for communicating with people. Whether they're empaths or not. (And whether other people are empaths? Not your business, anyway.)

Could you delve deeply into your feelings? Maybe locate a memory from your "formative years"? Or pull out your inner thesaurus to find 18 different words to describe every minute particle of emotional pain?

Sure you could. But don't.

Your empath coach now repeats, "Don't." Why not?

Because you won't solve problems by overwhelming other people with all this info. In fact, you may know a fine acronym that could — with all respect — have been designed for an empath like you: TMI. (Meaning "Too Much Information.")

End with a Practical Solution in Objective Reality

Many problems that bother empaths, really annoying problems ... They can be solved by referring to simple, objective things. Such as spoons, personal belongings, money, physical bodies, what a person literally says and does.

And Please, Please Leave This Out

Anything else.

Why leave out anything else? Because, Brave Explorer, this Communication Formula has an elegant simplicity. Bringing you the best results with nothing extra added.

So, please:

- No boundary talk. (That's a different technique, and one that may have served its purpose for you. Perhaps leading, now, only to diminishing returns. And definitely outside the scope of this 30-Day Plan for Empath Empowerment.)
- No apologizing. You have the right to solve problems. So don't undercut your good, objective communication by whimpering, etc.
- No adding energetic fixes. Perhaps you've heard of the Golden Bubble technique. Or other forms of visualization that supposedly will cure all ills *energetically*. By all means, go onto my blog and search on "Golden Bubble." There you can learn, in lavish detail, why energy fixes like that are worse than a waste of time.
- Less is more. At least when it comes to our shiny, new Communication Formula. A few short sentences will work best.

Your Assignment for Day 17

Brave Explorer, your assignment today is to use our Formula for Better Communication in your personal life. Use it as appropriate.

What if your relationships are so perfect that you have no need for this kind of problem solving? Then do a remote run on people you observe having problems. Here's what I mean.

Suppose that you're watching a movie at home. Where a scene shows a downtrodden spouse being bullied by his significant other. Turn off the show and practice. Taking the role of that spouse, speak up on his behalf.

1. **When you scream at me,**
2. **I feel embarrassed.**
3. **Please talk to me in a normal tone of voice. Otherwise don't say anything at all.**

Of course, do this kind of practice only in private. Likewise, do not, under any circumstances, use our Formula for Better Communication on a work relationship. At least, not until you have practiced using this new skill many times… and you're ready to take the consequences.

Skilled empaths don't shoot ants with cannons. Using your power in the objective world — for many empaths, that is a very new approach to solving problems. Developing skill takes a bit of practice.

But you probably need no practice at all to know this is true for you: In the subjective realm you were born powerful.

Go forth today, Brave Explorers. Start using your power in the objective realm, too.

DAY 18

Gusto

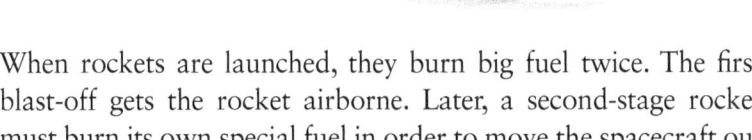

When rockets are launched, they burn big fuel twice. The first blast-off gets the rocket airborne. Later, a second-stage rocket must burn its own special fuel in order to move the spacecraft out of the earth's atmosphere.

Consider this a perfect analogy for your progress at becoming The Most Important Person in The Room. Becoming a skilled empath, you have two phases for blasting off into freedom. Phase One involved your first enthusiasm over Empath Empowerment.

Wow! Boom! You had liftoff!

This flashy phase was fueled by self-discovery. Receiving those first easy benefits of starting this 30-Day Program, maybe you were tempted to think that you understood everything right away.

Therefore, dilettantes and superficial learners will have quit reading this book by now. But not you, Brave Explorer. I can tell because you're still here with me.

That means you have moved forward enough for your second-stage rocket, Phase Two. It is fueled by determination to live the benefits of Empath Empowerment.

To move forward, you need to release a second-stage rocket by blasting through *deep* resistance.

Not just the pesky resistance that was covered on Intellect Day. But a deeper kind of resistance, a hidden obstacle that all empaths must move through before becoming truly skilled.

Blast off Bigger

Why would deep resistance be a factor? Empath Empowerment involves more than concepts, techniques and homework assignments, much as (I know that) you love them. (Ha! Sarcasm is allowed again today.)

What if you have been living mainly through one of the seven categories of Advanced Bingo? For instance:

- All emotions, all the time — that's my motto.
- Everything can be understood through my intellect (supposedly).
- Spirituality has me living higher than Rapunzel's tower

What's wrong with feeling or thinking that full-blooded earth reality is beneath you? Nothing... in theory. Everything... in habit.

Remember that classic line from the movie called "The Sixth Sense"? A psychic boy, played by Haley Joel Osment, tells his psychologist, played by Bruce Willis, "I see dead people.... Walking around like regular people. They don't see each other. They only see what they want to see. They don't know they're dead."

Not for a moment does it occur to the Bruce Willis character that he might be among the clueless dead.

Well, discovering that you've been trapped in just one category (e.g., emotions, intellect or spirit) can be a shock. Not as bad as learning, like Bruce, that you're a ghost! More like hearing from a kind friend that you've got bad breath.

Fortunately, there can be a sweet-smelling solution to any of these problems of emphasis for human life, a solution at least as thrilling as walking on the moon. It's called LIVING ON EARTH WITH GUSTO.

Skeptical that you might have hidden resistance to living on earth? Here's a recent client story to illustrate how empaths can be stuck without knowing it.

Using Metaphysics to Remain Stuck

Years ago Suzanne asked me for an Aura Report. This is a service I no longer offer, preferring to do full sessions with clients, not just give introductory samples. Back in the day, though, I offered brief readings where my client would send a photo. Then I'd email back info about seven different chakra databanks, summarizing what I learned about gifts of the soul and STUFF.

Put as tactfully as possible, Suzanne's Aura Report revealed that she wasn't living with much balance. Her Third Eye Chakra databanks about spirituality were vastly bigger than other parts of her aura. Suzanne took the news well. Months later, she scheduled an appointment.

"Woo-hoo," I thought. "Using techniques of RES Energy HEALING, I can help Suzanne to remove large amounts of STUFF, which will help her rebalance."

But no, Suzanne wanted a session of RES Energy READING instead. Granted, she had prepared beautifully, listing research items of interest. Unfortunately, all of them were about spirituality, like doing yoga or practicing Reiki or reading spiritual books.

In keeping with Suzanne's request, I supplied detailed feedback. Repeatedly I described how her big growth area was *everything but* the spiritual practices that enthralled her. "Please pay attention to other aspects of your life," I pleaded.

After several months, Suzanne contacted me again. She wanted a new Aura Report to validate all the progress she was making. I asked her to consider instead some Energy HEALING. But no. Suzanne felt convinced that visualizations, prayers, etc. had made all the difference in the world. She wanted me to describe her vastly strengthened aura.

Alas, Suzanne's aura was just as stuck as before. Afterwards she emailed me, "Oh well, I guess I should have taken your advice and applied the fee for this Aura Report toward a session of Energy

HEALING. I don't think I know what it feels like to be grounded."

Hey, I'm rooting for Suzanne. Her willingness to choose healing next time suggests that, in her own way, she is overcoming resistance to change. (Except I should note that 10 years after first-drafting this chapter, here I am editing merrily away when I realize that, oops! Suzanne still hasn't scheduled that session.)

Anyway, let's find out right now if you have been dealing with deep resistance to living on earth. For every one of our Cast of Characters who is an empath, there can be a different kind of deep resistance. Some examples follow. Can you recognize yourself in any of the descriptions that follow?

Stuckness #1. The Feeling Life

Zachary is more sensitive than he looks. Unless with trusted friends, he keeps quiet. When he does talk, mostly it's about emotions:

- Who is good, who isn't — based on Zachary's emotions
- How today goes, based on Zachary's emotions
- Personal growth, in terms of Zachary's emotions

Is anything wrong with being so emotionally aware? Nothing, except for being oblivious to all the other categories of Zachary's **MBS. I See.**

How much does Zachary learn from what happens in his environment (a.k.a., objective life events)? Unless major drama ensues, Zachary notices only emotions.

Physical body — has that been glimpsed recently? Sorta. You see, Zachary cares only about how he feels about that body.

Could there be mindfulness? Sure, if it counts that Zachary is mostly mindful of his emotions. (Except, oops, that has nothing to do with his mind.)

Intellectual activity? Being a bright guy, Zachary can tell you precisely how he *feels* about different ideas.

Spiritual life? Ask Zachary and he'll gladly tell you his feelings about religion and spirituality.

Soul expression? To Zachie, "soul" whatever makes him feel emotionally "positive," nothing more.

Your Assignment for Day 18. If you are like Zachary

What will help you move into a fuller experience of life? Go back to Days 7-14. Do each of these chapters in turn, one day at a time. Except skip Day 10, Emotions Day. Be proud of the A+ you've already earned there.

Why repeat the assignments for all those days? It's not that last time you did the assignments wrong. You're just becoming capable of doing them better. And here's the one thing I want you to add this time around: Gusto.

While you're enjoying your experience of Body Day, etc., congratulate yourself often. Tell yourself, "Ooh la la." (Substitute your favorite term for gusto.) Basically, you're reminding yourself, "This aspect of life is good. I can enjoy myself here."

Stuckness #2. All Figured Out

Hannah is such a brain. She has figured out just about everything. And everyone. Now that she understands all our previous chapters about Empath Empowerment, she may be tempted to skim through the rest of the book and not bother doing the exercises.

Big mistake, Hannah! According to an old proverb, "The eyes can see everything but the eyes." Likewise, mighty though Hannah's brain may be, her intellect cannot warn her about getting stuck in her intellect. (Brave Explorer, can you relate?)

But there's hope. Hannah can recognize her problem by reading the following:

Participating in her social environment, Hannah's an expert. She can psych out any conversation, deconstructing power struggles with ease and supplying the subtexts for every speaker. After a conversation, Hannah can easily summarize all she has learned. But does she ever make human contact without bringing along that detached figure-out-er? Maybe not.

Physical body present? If you ask Hannah to notice her body, she can tell you plenty. Oboy, so much she can tell you — about her health, or maybe medical facts, or how a person should eat properly. Alas, feeling sensations within her own body is another story, seemingly trivial.

Would her mind be of interest? Hannah definitely gets the concept of mind. So what's new and interesting about that? Clearly the world "interesting" doesn't apply to her mind, with its dull recycling of concepts Hannah has known, like, forever. Boring!

Emotions anyone? Emotional intelligence may be a point of pride for Hannah. Naming emotions for anyone, herself included, Hannah displays brilliant accuracy. But how about experiencing an emotion directly without analyzing it? That's for babies, right?

Spiritual life is a snap. Hannah may think herself quite the authority. Alternatively, she may have decided that spirituality is a fuzzy ideal, and simplistic. Either way, Hannah could be plenty evolved. Yet she will remain a cosmic underachiever... so long as she lives in her head.

What does it mean to express her soul? For Hannah, "soul" means "thinking about things." And that's all, for her, for now. Only "soul" could mean a whole lot more. The following assignment can help make that happen.

Your Assignment for Day 18. If you are like Hannah

What could help you to blast beyond deep resistance? Go back to Days 7-14. Do each of these chapters in turn, one day at a time, except skip Day 9, Intellect Day.

Resisting that assignment? Look, you know you're smart. Everybody who knows you… gets that. Well, folks will respect you even more when you use categories of yourself beyond that mighty brain.

So often, what do people do when stuck? We try *harder*, rather than *differently*. Well, here comes your exercise in "differently." Last time you did Days 7-14 just fine. This time I invite you to re-do these chapters and learn nothing new whatsoever.

Imagine, no intellectual discoveries required. Instead, be sloppy and silly and go for pure gusto. Which means what, exactly? While you're enjoying your experience of Body Day, etc., congratulate yourself. Say "Eureka!" (Substitute your favorite term for gusto.) Remind yourself, "I can relax and enjoy myself here. Afterwards I'll still be smart."

Stuckness #3. Going Spiritual

Back to our analogy about lifting off with a second-stage rocket, unless the launch site is stable, you can't go anywhere. A strong platform is needed to thrust against. Unfortunately, James has never valued that platform.

God love him, James is such a devoted spiritual seeker. He neglects everything else but spirit, forgetting that Earth School was created the way it is for a reason. Every component of his mind-body-spirit-intellect-soul-emotions-environment is valuable for spiritual evolution.

Therefore, even for the sake of his service to others as a skilled empath, James needs to overcome his comforting old tendency to "go spiritual."

I'm a good one to help with this problem because I spent more than two straight decades that way, addicted to going spiritual whenever possible. Everything had to be about God… or my spiritual search… or my belief system.

Brave Explorer, can you, too, can identify with James' way of being stuck, sweetly stuck in over-enthusiastic spiritual seeking.

But what about evolving through human experiences in the environment, objective reality? James wants to *evolve*, not get *involved*. Thus, he struggles to find meaning, substituting that for getting a life.

Everything happens for a reason, supposedly. For James, life itself can't be trusted, nor can his own instincts about making choices (supposedly). Instead, everyday existence is treated like a test. And James' assignment is to figure out what on earth he's supposed to learn. Maybe his angels could tell him? Maybe a psychic?

Why care about that physical body? It's such a downer. If James could choose, he would banish forever that silly, boring "vehicle." Maybe he does the next best thing and neglects it. Or maybe James works really hard to perfect his body, eating only the purest of vegan foods, doing yoga, etc. Either way, it's not much fun for James, having that body.

How about his mind, that very human Mecca? If James' spiritual path emphasizes mindfulness, he'll strive for it. Otherwise, he'll neglect that mind completely. Since being mentally present is a very human enterprise, and James prefers godly, not human.

Having emotions, could that be worthwhile? *Interpreting* those emotions seems much more rewarding. James may even have developed the habit of translating emotions just as fast as they happen, completely bypassing direct feelings. Why not?

Depending on his belief system, James has the perfect label to define any emotion, explain it away or deny it. Indeed, feeling emotions directly — without extra labeling — might be considered "unspiritual" or "un-evolved."

In his active pursuit of the spiritual, does James find much of a role for intellectual activity? Depends! Possibly he employs the intellect mostly to interpret experience in terms of his belief system. Perhaps James belongs to a "Movement" or church that has taught him preferred ways to speak of worldly things. Certainly, James prefers to bring any conversation around to his favorite topic, the spiritual. Is this really as intellectually adventurous as it seems, or more like playing one favorite song again and again?

As for soul, his soul expression in this lifetime, what about expressing that? Ironically, James is more at risk for neglecting his soul than somebody who doesn't go spiritual. Why? He works so hard at what he believes is all that matters. By contrast, expressing your soul means honoring your human likes and dislikes, catching a spark that interests you and fanning it into a flame through doing more, more, more. But James mistrusts spontaneity.

Your Assignment for Day 18. If you are like James

What could help a big seeker like you to overcome deep resistance? Go back to Days 7-14. Do each of these chapters in turn, one day at a time, except skip Day 11, Spiritual Awareness Day. You've worked heroically hard at that part and, yes, you can be sure that God notices.

Why repeat the other chapters? It's not that last time you did them wrong. You're just becoming capable of doing them better. And here's the one thing I want you to do differently this time around: Gusto.

When you're enjoying your experience of body, etc., congratulate yourself. Say "Praise Jesus." (Substitute your favorite term for gusto.) Immediately afterwards, delve into the experience, as if human life really mattered. Remember, "This aspect of life is sacred or God never would have created it. So it's spiritually safe for me to surrender to my human experience. And enjoy it."

No Problem

Whew! You've read through three descriptions of deep resistance and can proudly say you don't have them. Excellent!

Also, give yourself credit for not making life all about your physical body. Even though some empaths have just one physical gift, Physical Intuition or Physical Oneness, I haven't yet encountered a single empath who focuses only on physical life. Mysterious!

What explains that? My theory is this: All empaths, whatever their gifts, have been born way too evolved to believe "I am my physical body."

Take your own survey. Ask any empath you know, "Do you believe that mainly you are your physical body?"

Anyway, you don't believe that, do you? You are an increasingly balanced combo of mind-body-spirit-intellect-soul-emotions-environment. And, therefore, you can progress from this page onward without having to repeat a single previous chapter.

Your Assignment for Day 18. Not stuck in any category

Look, you still could have deep resistance to fully living in the world as The Most Important Person in The Room. Let's find out how easy it is for you, doing today's assignment.

- Add gusto. Continue being The Most Important Person in The Room and do it unapologetically, enthusiastically.
- Continue to turn your empath gift(s) OFF whenever you notice that you have a choice. (And make it your business to notice when you have that choice.)
- Use the "Take It" technique to keep other people's pain from becoming your business. Yet still bring them help.
- The Hello technique will also help you stay clear of other people's pain.
- Finally, direct your consciousness, Being Deep, to continue your lifelong education in gusto.

Gusto is the basis of Empath Empowerment.

DAY 19

Pass the Test

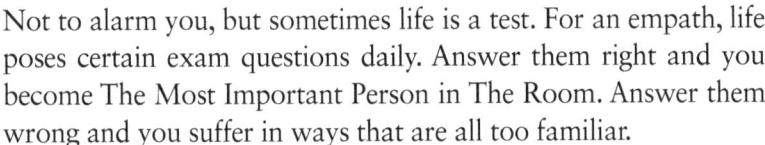

Not to alarm you, but sometimes life is a test. For an empath, life poses certain exam questions daily. Answer them right and you become The Most Important Person in The Room. Answer them wrong and you suffer in ways that are all too familiar.

Day by day, you have been gaining skill at using your consciousness to ace that test. I'm very proud of you, Brave Explorer.

Underlying beliefs will keep you motivated (or not) to succeed completely with our 30-Day Plan, adding the rest of the skills needed for Empath Empowerment. Let's assess those relevant beliefs in today's Values Quiz.

Values Quiz

Choose A or B to finish each statement.

1. *What is good about being born as an empath:*

A. Nothing. You're just meant to suffer.

B. Plenty. You have great opportunities to learn about people and help them.

2. *The main benefit of being an empath is:*

A. You can gain enormous wisdom while serving other people brilliantly.

B. Bragging rights are the point. Tell everybody you know who isn't an empath, "I'm more special."

3. *How you can stop connecting to others super-deeply (just out of habit):*

A. Cover up your problems with big, fake "boundaries" or an artificial "invisible shield." Or constantly analyze the STUFF you have taken on -- does it originally belong to yourself or to others?

B. Use skill to turn your empath gift(s) OFF. Then your gift(s) will remain, fresh and fine, available to use whenever you actively decide to turn the inner switch ON. As for STUFF belonging to others, it won't be there, period.

4. *The key to using your empath gift(s) safely is:*

A. Develop the habit of keeping your gift(s) turned OFF as a matter of routine. To turn your gift(s) ON, use a safe technique. Otherwise, don't bother. Long term, you'll pay a heavy price for any insights.

B. Introduce yourself to people this way, "I'm Pat and I'm an empath. That means I'm weak and whiny, with a terrible psychic-level disability. Watch my vlog and see me being vulnerable. Then weep along with me!"

5. *Is it okay to turn my empath gift(s) OFF most of the time?*

A. No, since I have no right to take care of myself. Whenever I'm in the room with another person, that means I'm supposed to give. If I'm burned out, this is because of my fate.

B. Yes, of course I can turn my gift(s) OFF. I could even consider this an investment in helping others. Being rested and balanced as a person, I'll give better service whenever I actively choose to turn my empath gift(s) ON.

It's better to really help one person each day than to walk around tired and cranky, giving to everyone who crosses my path… and giving with only 2% clarity.

6. What does burnout mean to an empath?

A. Feeling burned out is a reminder to turn my gift(s) OFF. Hey, when people have problems, I am hardly the only empath or healer available.

B. Burnout represents wonderful proof of how special I am. Besides, paying attention to myself rather than others would make me selfish. To me, what does exhaustion mean? "Drink more coffee."

7. The very idea that I could position my consciousness purposely as a skilled empath... brings up this reaction within me:

A. Hooray! I can learn to do that. The main way to turn my gift(s) OFF is an occasional, super-easy tweak to my consciousness.

There are so many categories: **MBS. I See.** Directing my consciousness can help me to access them all.

B. Sob, who me? Aim my consciousness? That wouldn't be fair. I have zero rights about doing things purposely.

If other people could possibly benefit even slightly from my help, their needs matter far more than mine. Obviously, everyone else in the universe is far more powerful, important, good looking, smells better, etc.

8. Guilt over turning my gift(s) OFF means that:

A. I am a good person and, possibly, saintly. The guiltier I feel, the more worthy am I.

B. Could be, I need some emotional or spiritual energy healing. Maybe I can do that healing on my own. Otherwise, if I need professional help, I'll make it my business to get some.

9. Other people I know don't yet have the kind of skills I am developing. Therefore:

A. Really, I ought to wait until everyone else is doing this Empath Empowerment thing before I fully commit. Until then, I'll use this book for light reading.

Honestly, instead of using these 30 days to become a skilled empath, instead of doing the daily assignments, I could make important investments in my popularity through more active participation in Instagram.

B. Who cares? If I don't advocate for my own happiness, nobody else will. Each person is responsible for his or her own life.

10. *The worst thing that could happen if I turn OFF my gift(s) as an empath is:*

A. My friends could die. I am the only savior.

B. I'll stop enabling people who have been stuck. Wait, that isn't so horrible — especially because everyone has access to God, everyone can choose to grow or not, and saving other adults has never been my responsibility at all.

11. *Okay, the VERY worst thing that could happen if I turn my empath gift(s) off would be:*

A. God will hate me and remove every bit of my sensitivity forever.

B. Nothing.

Answers

Come on, you know which answers are correct.

If you can't figure it out on your own (and even if you can), try our next technique.

Inner Research

This technique for Inner Research is a great way to get guidance from within, guidance from your mind-body-spirit-intellect-soul-emotions. The environment portion relates to wherever you are doing the technique, sitting comfortably, paying attention to yourself.

Let's use Inner Research to experiment with the Values Quiz you just did.

1. Close your eyes and notice how you feel.
2. Open your eyes. Choose any question you like from this quiz. Read any answer provided. Repeat the memorable parts in your head, thinking this slowly inside as if you were chewing it with your mind.
3. Close your eyes. Take a couple of deep breaths. Notice how you feel.
4. Open your eyes. Sort out the meaning of what you've just experienced.

Yes, your feelings count, whether they come from your physical body, your emotions, your spirit… any category of who you are. Every choice, viewed with Inner Research will bring forth inner experience, feelings included. That information is valuable.

You Can Trust That Inner Research

Brave Explorer, I trust you to make the A-or-B choices in line with becoming empowered as an empath.

Yet maybe some feelings surprised you while doing Inner Research? For instance, you researched Question #6 and got to "Burnout represents wonderful proof of how special I am." Theoretically, you knew this answer is wrong. Yet perhaps, doing Inner Research, you felt differently, more along the lines of, "Ooh, but I really enjoy the martyrdom."

Consider any unexpected information valuable.

To put this another way, don't deny any problems that pop up courtesy of our Inner Research. Use your favorite resources for quality energy healing or therapy.

Don't let the prospect of personal growth overwhelm you. Remember, you've got the power of your conscious mind, your subconscious mind, God, and many top-notch helpers of various kinds in the world who could help you, if asked.

Your Assignment for Day 19

Let's continue the usual tactics to keep you turning your empath gift(s) OFF:

1. Should problems arise in Objective Reality, do your best to solve them on the objective level.
2. Sometimes Your Formula for Better Communication will do the trick.
3. Other times you'll need to figure out some other strategy.
4. Just keep in mind the idea of communication. Which sure beats living in your head while experiencing or imagining what it's like to be someone else.
5. Any time you're bored, play Advanced Bingo.
6. And, sure, Be Deep occasionally.

DAY 20

Hold a Space

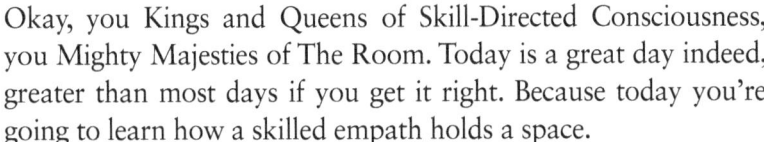

Okay, you Kings and Queens of Skill-Directed Consciousness, you Mighty Majesties of The Room. Today is a great day indeed, greater than most days if you get it right. Because today you're going to learn how a skilled empath holds a space.

I'm reasonably certain this will be way different from what you've been doing before.

What does it mean to HOLD A SPACE? Whenever you pay attention to another person, you have a way of positioning your consciousness. That way of holding a space can be changed, much as everyday habits with breathing can be changed. Provided that you want to experiment.

Unskilled empaths habitually hold a space differently from non-empaths. We get closer. Compounding that, we often do unskilled empath merges, whooshing in and out of the other person's auric field. Unless we know better, we don't call this "How I hold a space" but rather "Getting comfortable with another person" or even "Being normal."

Ha, normal for somebody who picks up pain! (A.k.a. Imported STUFF.)

Of course, you have habits for holding a space. You also have choices. Here's an analogy from the body language specialty called "proxemics." People from different cultures grow up learning to hold others at a certain *physical* distance. For instance, Italians stand closer than Germans.

Regardless of upbringing, however, you can consciously choose to change your habits with physical distance. Despite being of Italian descent, you can train yourself to stand farther apart, more like a German. Similarly, you can change your comfort zone with inner space. This really matters for empaths.

Holding a Space

Let's refine the concept of holding a space. Already you know this means how close you get to a person by means of consciousness. Did you also know this? Holding a space differs from merely paying attention. Why? Because it involves positioning consciousness.

YOU: Would you please pay attention while I'm talking to you?

TROY: I'm paying attention perfectly fine.

YOU: No way. You're texting. You're tweeting. You're barely listening to me.

TROY: What, you want me to repeat back the very last things you said? I could.

See the point, Brave Explorer? Troy may pay attention just fine (by his standards) yet still not hold a space for you at all. (The technical term for this, as you'll soon read, is "Space Dial Set at 1.") Clues about paying attention show in body language, and this is completely separate from what happens with consciousness.

Jocelyn, in the same room with Troy and you, might seem completely disconnected from your conversation. Yet energetically she could be intimately involved with both of you. (And, sadly, doing unskilled empath merges galore.)

You'd have to read auras to tell what was going on… or else do a Skilled — not unskilled — Empath Merge.

No wonder far more people know about paying attention versus what happens with holding a space.

You, however, have developed the perfect background for exploring this topic. What prepared you, exactly? Some techniques you were given on previous days, like Be Deep; these actively used your consciousness. Today you will learn how to take that further, exercising a very subtle kind of muscle.

Normally, this muscle works all by itself but you can also move it on purpose, just like the fine muscles under your eyes. Have you ever figured out how to round your eyes or narrow them? Then you can surely play with how you hold a space.

Consciousness Muscles

Right now I'm preparing you for a technique you'll do soon. Both this preparation and what follows… they're not for browsers. Please, don't just read this. Do it. Otherwise, read the rest of this chapter later. Since, Brave Explorer, for your first encounter, I want you to enjoy a full-force, virginal, inner Aha!

At this point in teaching you, I'll use the term "Space Dial" but won't explain it much until you have had some direct, personal experience. Hey, you've already had 19 days to learn to trust me, so please trust me on this.

A Human Resource

Preparing for this next technique, you'll need one of the following options, listed in order of best choice first:

- A friend who is physically in the room with you, someone who agrees to be part of your experiment. He or she must also agree to do a couple of techniques with you in silence, without giggling, complaining, texting, etc. (Hey, your friend has the rest of his/her life for all that.)
- A photograph of someone you're fond of. This picture must show just this one person, and from a front angle. The photo must also be large enough to show the person's face clearly. Electronic pix are fine, BTW.

- A magazine or newspaper photo of a stranger, such as a fashion model. For our experiment to work, this head shot must be from a front angle and be large enough to show the face and neck clearly. Also, yes, by "person" I do mean somebody human. Cat gazing would be a different exercise.

On A Practical Note

For planning purposes, a friend makes an ideal person for doing the techniques in this chapter. When you issue your invitation, please know that you're going to be doing a couple of different techniques together, so allow for 30-45 minutes. First you'll be exploring consciousness with that partner; then you'll be reading and thinking on your own. Next, you'll be doing another exploration with that same person. (Maybe arrange to thank that person, bartering a favor in return.)

Practice the Position

Next let's practice your physical position. Let me play choreographer and you be the dancer, okay? Then, as I list the following dance steps, don't substitute trying to get into the mood of the dance. Physically go through the motions, knowing that we are practicing position, not yet doing the full technique to Hold a Space.

- With a friend, sit opposite each other on chairs, spaced with 6-12 inches between your knees. From now on, I'll refer to this person as your "**DISCOVERY PERSON.**"
- Otherwise, with a photo, sit comfortably. Hold up the photo so that you can see it on the level, as if it were a real person's face sitting across from yours. And yes, I'll also refer to this individual as your Discovery Person.

Do the Alternating Sequence

For this little technique, we'll practice an Alternating Sequence, a kind of Peek-a-Boo for grownups. Then:

1. Glance at one part of your partner's face (except avoid the eyes).
2. Then look away at something else in the room (like a wall).
3. Glance at one part of your partner's body (like one shoulder).
4. Look at something else in the room (like a chair).
5. Alternate looking at your Discovery Person and looking at something else in the room. Always avoid your Discovery Person's eyes.

How to pace your looking? Choose any speed you prefer, fast or slow. Just give equal time to both halves of the Alternating Sequence, seeing your partner and looking away.

Now, Brave Explorer, you're ready for a fuller technique.

Meet Your Space Dial

Your Space Dial is a faculty within you for holding a space. Now let's explore it. Read through the following instructions, then do them step by step.

1. Close your eyes. Take a deep breath. Notice how it feels to be you right now. (Yes, this is like our earlier exercise to Be Deep.)
2. Then notice in a second way how it feels to be you. (Yes, this is like playing Advanced Bingo. Choose a different category of Mind-Body-Spirit. Intellect. Soul-emotions-environment.)
3. Get Big. Think the name "God," or another name that you'd prefer as your highest source of Divine inspiration. (One quick thought does it. You're connected.)
4. Set an intention with this quick thought, "I'm ready to learn more about myself."
5. Open your eyes. Then do the Alternating Sequence for about two minutes.

6. Close your eyes. Take a deep breath. Notice how it feels to be you right now, using both of the two categories you explored before. Do you feel any different now? Ask this question in a simple, undemanding way. Just as simply, accept each answer.
7. Open your eyes. Technique Time over.

So, what was that like for you? Whether or not you notice any change is no big deal. Please, avoid using any self-interrogation techniques that might, or might not, be considered torture.

Add More Finesse at Using Your Space Dial

Congratulations on all you've learned so far from exploring your Space Dial. Next I'll help you learn more. Meanwhile, if you've got a live Discovery Person, invite him/her to wait in another room while you study a bit more, since you'll soon have more to do together. (Of course, don't share anything about this book, and your personal 30-Day Plan, with your Discovery Person.)

Brave Explorer, since childhood you've developed habits for holding a space with another person. Habits of an unskilled empath, actually. So you're used to turning that Space Dial all the way ON to the maximum setting; a shocking idea perhaps, but very likely.

Here's some perspective. For years I've researched how different people hold a space, doing Skilled Empath Merges on a wide variety of people, using techniques like the one you'll learn on Day 28. Having conducted hundreds of these experiments in consciousness, I'm convinced that empaths and non-empaths have radically different ways of holding a space.

Unskilled empaths hold a space with great intimacy. By comparison, when non-empaths hold a space… they treat other people more like objects. (Not to worry, this way of living is equally valuable for spiritual evolution, given intrinsic differences between non-empaths and empaths.) Maybe you're wondering, what does it mean to experience somebody like an object? Surely you've seen it happen:

- Say that you go to a speed-dating event where singles are being looked up and down, scrutinized like food at the meat market. Should you walk in there with a super-buff body, suitably groomed and dressed, you will be treated as a **SEX OBJECT**.
- Imagine a family reunion, where you're part of a large family. Out of the whole bunch, you happen to be the only one who has managed to get rich. To your family, you may no longer seem like a person. Instead, you're somebody to ask for a loan. Or a gift. Or a future inheritance. Goodbye person, hello **MONEY OBJECT**.
- Finally, picture that you're in college, where it's easy for you to excel, given your genius I.Q. and excellent study habits. Congratulations! Except some kids make friends with you for ulterior motives. They don't want your company so much as they desire free tutoring. In short, to them, you're a **BRAIN OBJECT**.

Granted, these are extreme examples. But in everyday life, non-empaths often view other people more or less as objects, as shown in the Space Dial illustration on our next page. Non-empaths naturally have a default of Space Dial set at 1.

Every Human Alive Has a Space Dial.

But do we all use it in the same way? Definitely not! Because non-empaths usually keep their Space Dial set at 1; compared to you they're relate to other people more like objects. Please understand, Brave Explorer, this doesn't make them bad people, narcissists, ets. It's just how the majority of human beings live.

Narcissists have no desire to ever turn their Space Dial higher. By contrast, non-empaths prize moving it higher. But how much higher? That's an interesting question.

Space Dial OFF

- A non-empath trying to get close to another person might spontaneously turn that Space Dial up to 3.
- A non-empath who falls in love will spontaneously move that Space Dial up to a 4.
- Taking care of one's baby, a non-empath might automatically move that Space Dial as high as a 4.
- A non-empath having sex might manage a temporary turn-on of that Space Dial all the way up to 5. Then, wham, bam! It's back to 1.

Maybe that's one reason why pop culture makes such a big deal of sex. Generations ago, people used to say of great sex, "The earth moved for me."

Then and now, sex just might represent a non-empath's best chance to move beyond having consciousness centered in his or her physical body.

Honestly, as an empath, you may have had great sex. Hope so! But did you ever feel that sex was the only time your consciousness moved far away from feeling bound by your physical body?

"The earth moved for me" is like saying, "That sexual experience was so powerful, it cause the sun to start orbiting the earth."

With greater perspective, we get it. Earth moves around the sun, not the other way around. Likewise, if your consciousness moves away from being localized in your physical body, that's not because your entire planet moved.

Back to the More Mundane Topic of Your Space Dial

Bold Explorer, when you did the previous exercise, you weren't asked to have sex. Look, I didn't even ask you to adjust your Space Dial. Automatically, then, your Space Dial was set at your usual default position. Probably at 10. (*See the illustration after you turn the page.*)

Space Dial ON

Now let's get some contrast going. Soon I'll ask you to do the Alternating Sequence with just one difference, compared to before.

This next time, when you alternate with your Discover Person, simply look at your him or her like just another piece of furniture.

Yes, Furniture

Please practice this furniture idea before we go fully into doing the technique.
1. Look around in the room where you are. You can see different objects, right? A lamp. A desk. A chair.
2. Look, at one object then move. Look at another, then on to the next.
3. Don't linger longer than five seconds on any one object. A brisk pace will help you remain on the surface.

Notice? You do have a way of looking at furniture! It doesn't walk or talk or breathe (unless it's a very expensive piece of furniture). So, empath or not, you know how to treat furniture as an inanimate object.

In our next technique, you'll get to treat your Discovery Person just the same way. Meat at the singles event! A brain in the genius-at-school fantasy! I call this variation on our Space Dial exercise "The Furniture Game." Weird though it may feel, do it anyway.

The Furniture Game

The steps are simple, Brave Explorer. Here goes:
1. Sit opposite your Discovery Person, at least several inches apart.
2. Close your eyes. Take a deep breath. Notice how it feels to be you right now.
3. Then notice in a second way how it feels to be you. (Choose a different category of Mind-Body-Spirit. Intellect. Soul-emotions-environment.)

4. Get Big. Think the name "God," or another name that you'd prefer to call on your highest source of inspiration. (One quick thought does it. You're connected.)
5. Set an intention with this quick thought, "I'm ready to learn more about myself."
6. Open your eyes. Do the Alternating Sequence for about two minutes. In this version, you will treat your partner like furniture.
7. Close your eyes. Take a deep breath. How does it feel to be you right now? Notice your first category chosen before, then your second category. Has anything about your inner experience shifted?

Did the Earth Move for You?

Please, put those clothes back on!

Seriously, now that you've played The Furniture Game, how was it different from when you did Meet Your Space Dial?

In particular, did the process change you as much? Think again about the comparison, being aware of yourself at the start vs. the end.

In my workshops, most students notice a difference immediately.

- With their Space Dials naturally turned up to 10, they tend to pick up Imported STUFF belonging to their partner.
- With their Space Dials turned down to 1, they don't.
- Can you relate?

Before You Continue With this Learning Process...

Go ahead and thank your Discovery Person. Full credit has been earned for doing you a favor! And now back to you and what you've just done.

But-But-But

If we were in a workshop together, by now, at least one of your classmates would be raising a hand to complain:

"I may have felt better, but it scared me, turning my Space Dial down to 1."

How about you? Did you fear one any of these possibilities?

- The other person might notice.
- The other person might think you are selfish.
- The other person might die from lack of attention.

Actually, none of this happens, especially that death part. Remember, most people are non-empaths. And since they keep their Space Dials at 1 most of the time, when you go from 10 to 1, how would they know the difference?

You can safely adapt your new skill with The Furniture Game , adapting to real-life social situations, whether it's hanging out with your roommate or discretely watching strangers on a bus.

This technique is meant to be used with eyes open. Just avoid doing it while multi-tasking, like talking to somebody while you adjust your Space Dial.

Multi-Tasking with Consciousness

Yes, there's a name for that. "Multi-Tasking with Consciousness." A common thing that people do these days. As if it's not enough to simply talk with another person. But instead you're doing something extra with your consciousness, taking an inner journey.

Like, maybe, asking yourself, "What's really going on with Zachary?" Or "Lexi doesn't seem interested. I wonder why not."

Sure people have always had fleeting thoughts and feelings while talking to others. But many of us living today — empaths included — are practically doing the equivalent of a Hamlet monologue, even while ostensibly in the midst of a real-life conversation.

Soon You Can Establish a New Habit

With daily practice, Brave Explorer, you can quickly grow comfortable with a new default position on your Space Dial: The habitual position of 1. Not 10, and nor 6 or even 2. Not for most social relationships.

Build that habit, day by day. Spending more and more time at that lowest setting on your Space Dial. Start in a coffee shop, looking at strangers. Eventually you'll hang out with a friend at that coffee shop. Always with your Space Dial *comfortably* set at 1.

Yes, comfortably. Beware the "comfort" that really is habit, where it feels "so natural" to emphasize the other person with your consciousness, even if you wind up feeling pretty awful afterward. With your Space Dial at 1, guess what? You'll pay more attention to what your friend actually says and does. In objective reality!

Here's another perspective that may help you. As you've already learned during our 30-Day Plan, it's good to aim for being The Most Important Person in The Room. That way you won't take on Imported STUFF.

Well, that's the same thing as keeping your Space Dial at 1, which really can become second nature, your default position. And guess what else? You may find that you have more energy, less often feeling physically tired. Because it take a lot out of a human being to keep that Space Dial too high, too much of the time. After you establish this habit, you can let your Space Dial fluctuate to any other setting. That's safe to do, once your default has become 1.

Simply Change How You Look at People

Here comes some extra help for *setting your Space Dial at 1 as a default*. The way that you physically look at people can make it far easier to turn down that Space Dial.

For the next few days, avoid direct eye contact with other people. You see, Brave Explorer, what happens when a person makes eye contact with somebody else? Both people's Space Dials usually zoom right up to the highest setting available for that individual. Meaning: For a non-empath it's 3. Whereas for you? More like 10.

In real life, how can you avoid eye contact if another person expects it of you? For the next few days, experiment with our next technique.

Eye Option #1

To protect yourself from involuntarily turning up your Space Dial, look in the eye *area*, not directly at the other person's eyes. For example, when with Lexi:

- Can you look at her forehead?
- Or one of her eyebrows?
- Or one of her ears?
- Sure can!

And most likely she won't know the difference.

By using Eye Option #1 exclusively for 3-5 days, you will strengthen your core sense of self.

Following that, you'll be ready for Eye Option #2, a second alternative to staring deeply into other people's eyes.

Eye Option #2

In a social situation where eye contact seems required, take only a super-quick glance at the other person's eyes. That would be one second or less.

Immediately move your eyes over slightly, to the eye *area*. Why the big rush, just one second?

Say that it's summer and your feet are bare. Until now, you have been standing on a nice, cool lawn. But now you must quickly walk down a bit of pavement. Man, but that's hot!

So you walk really fast. Do the same thing now, only with eyeballs. Skitter across that slightly dangerous territory.

When you stare eye-to-eye for two seconds or more, you won't risk burning your body. But you will risk turning your Space Dial up to 10, out of habit.

So don't. One second is plenty to make sure that Lexi still has two eyes, they're not rolled up in her head, no need to call an ambulance, etc.

Easy, isn't it? Losing your customary, automatic way of depth-gazing? That's no loss, considering the big gains you'll make as a person.

What if you're skeptical? Hey, you're on a 30-Day Plan, not a life sentence in Empath's Prison. Find out what this experiment can do for you. It just might improve your life in ways you can't yet imagine.

Fact is, you have a Range of Space Dial settings. Over time, you'll probably use 1-3 most often. Yet higher settings will be available to you for really important, sweet conversations. But what if a conversation turns troubling, so you need to solve problems in objective reality? Instantly, quite automatically, your Space Dial will turn down to setting 1,

How about letting your Space Dial go up to a 10 sometimes? Probably you'll reserve that powerful closeness for when you're doing a dedicated technique for Skilled Empath Merge. Like any wise person living now, in The Age of Awakening, you'll limit your total Technique Time to 20 minutes max, per day. Of course Skilled Empath Merge would count as Technique Time.

Well, what about all the hours you used to spend every day, drifting in and out of other people's auras? Unskilled empath merge added up to loads of Technique Time too, throwing a person out of balance. Fortunately, what you've learned today is going to help you, more than ever, to keep your empath gifts OFF. Except for when you purposely choose to do a Skilled Empath Merge.

The RANGE Available to You

Your Assignment for Day 20

Today is such an important day in your development as a skilled empath. When was the last day you discovered a new body part? Was it back when you were an infant, lying on your back and giggling uncontrollably as you played with your toes?

Like a part of your body — but in consciousness — that Space Dial is a subtle faculty within you. Here's how to profit from this tremendously important new discovery:

- Keep your Space Dial at 1 most of the time. (If a reminder is needed, give yourself a round of The Furniture Game in Social Situations.)
- If you're really itching to turn up your Space Dial a few times today, don't go higher than 3.
- Avoid looking people in the eye. Use Eye Option #1. Look at nearby parts of the face, rather than at the eyes themselves. After several days (at your discretion) you'll be ready for Eye Option #2 as well.
- The rest of today, see if you can have a couple of interactions with a real-live person. Non-texting, non-tweeting. Just human-type being with other people.
- Yes, it is possible. You could do some no-tech visiting, talking, smiling, sharing meals, etc. And while you do this, experiment with keeping that Space Dial at 1. Notice how, both during and after each interaction, you feel more like The Most Important Person in The Room.

Others are unlikely to notice, but you'll feel the difference.

DAY 21

Redefine Your Job

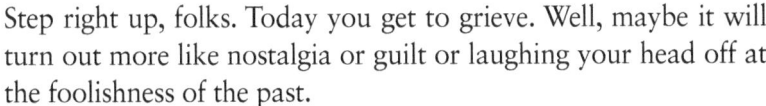

Step right up, folks. Today you get to grieve. Well, maybe it will turn out more like nostalgia or guilt or laughing your head off at the foolishness of the past.

Why? **Because** I'm going to help you gain extra skill at using your Space Dial. Yesterday, of course, was the Super-Duper, Inner High-Tech Day when you officially learned how to treat other people like furniture. I raised the shocking idea that non-empaths do this most of the time.

Even more shocking, you began actually doing that Furniture Game — I hope — which probably felt weird but strangely good.

If you followed through on your homework, you kept your Space Dial set at 1 for most of the day. So a reaction has probably set in, either grief or guilt or whatever.

Of course, your main reaction could have been positive. Did you notice subtle life-affirming emotions? Perhaps more self-confidence or greater self-compassion? (These are definitely going to be your long-term benefits from keeping that Space Dial at a default of 1.)

Unfortunately, you may not be used to paying attention to subtle life-affirming emotions, despite being very, very familiar with feelings like guilt.

So let's dedicate today to rehab. Think about it for a moment Which buttons did it push for you yesterday, turning down that Space Dial?

Next, a comforting thought. Today is Day 21 of our 30-Day Plan, compared to years when you probably lived with the equivalent of zero potty training. Apart from habit, there's no good reason to keep your Space Dial at 10, not if you want to live juicy as a person and also gain wisdom as a skilled empath, plus do a better job at helping others.

A Positive Change, Actually

Now hear this, whether or not you consciously noticed a lot of discomfort yesterday. Turning your empath gift(s) OFF means more than removing something, like turning your Space Dial down to a lower number.

Should it count as a loss, going from a big, heroic, self-sacrificing 10 to a puny 1? Oh, I think not. Whenever you turn that Space Dial down, you're turning up something else. Automatically you turn the mighty power of your consciousness toward *yourself*. Fascinating though you have been before, you're becoming way more fascinating… to yourself.

And, yes, this fascination may even turn contagious. Think of it like measles, only better looking. When you experience yourself as interesting — not just liking the concept, but living it — other people will most likely find you more interesting, too.

For sure, Brave Explorer, turning down that Space Dial means that something else automatically turns up. You become The Most Important Person in The Room, which means that you are more what?

Hmmm. Depends on What You Choose to Believe

What else can happen when you put yourself first? When you stick up for yourself? When you find yourself really, truly interesting?

Hey, I'm not here to dictate what all this will cause you to believe about yourself. Last time I checked, even God didn't dictate our personal feelings and thoughts.

But I do want to encourage you to use freedom of choice about what you believe. You could, for instance, choose to believe in yourself as someone important.

And that is a good thing! By contrast, certain popular beliefs in society are especially damaging to empaths, suggesting that "I do have value as a person" *but, but, but...*

- Men (or women) are like babies. For my love relationship to work, I must anticipate what my mate needs, then deliver it.
- Love means giving so much that it hurts.
- In order to be a good Christian (or devout follower of any religion), I must constantly sacrifice my own happiness.
- If I'm serious about my love relationship, I must maintain constant maximum-depth connection. Otherwise how will I know where I stand?
- It's my job to give like crazy whenever at work. After all, I'm a nurse, therapist, taxi driver, inmate escort at a prison, etc. (Fill in the blank with ANY profession.)
- When I was a child growing up with that alcoholic parent, Pat, I had to anticipate whatever Pat would do next; it was a matter of survival. Now, even though I'm no longer living in that dysfunctional family, I still feel safer if I keep all my empath circuits turned ON.

Why would such dismal beliefs serve you now? Maybe you find this short list of buts way too extreme. Yet you still feel guilty over turning down your Space Dial.

Maybe you have a fine civilized but, a small tasteful but... as it were. Which words, exactly, are inscribed on your but?

Ask yourself now, for pity's sake. And then ask yourself, "Why would this be true for me NOW?"

Because you're free to change. As a skilled empath, you can use your freedom of belief to provide some much needed wiggle room. And, eventually, a good life besides.

Better than those Buts

Let's take another look at our previous short list of buts. Aren't they really quite ridiculous? Here are examples of what you might substitute.

Sure, some men (and women) are like babies. But you don't have to choose a person like that to live with and be your love. Instead, you could choose a mate whose emotional age is older than two.

Definitely, love means giving so hard that it hurts... if you're dating the Marquis de Sade. If a demanding sadist is your idea of a desirable companion, you really might like to get out more.

In order to be a good Christian, etc. you must what? Please! Pull out your Bible or Book of Mormon or Upanishads or whatever and find me the quote. Is that grotesque suffering thing really, truly, required by your religion?

If ever you were taught such an atrocity, please, question the source. Was your "inspiration" a warped or power-hungry practitioner of some religion? Maybe someone well meaning. Maybe not!

For every suffering saint you know, there are plenty of happy members of that very same religion. They help others at least as much as the suffering sort. Plus they have way more fun.

Speaking of fun, what's the payoff for you to stay in a relationship where you must keep yourself so terribly vigilant? Is this relationship spelled L*O*V*E? Or, maybe, S*C*A*R*Y?

Yes, S*C*A*R*Y

About volunteering to do unskilled empath merges at work, are you kidding? As an empath, you may have assumed it's your job to give like crazy at work. If so, take a fresh look at people you meet who also work as nurses, therapists, guards at your nearest prison, etc.

Most are not empaths. (A statistical fact, right?) Therefore, when professionally trained, they were taught a skill set that was not based on being an empath. Yes, that is true even of nurses, psychotherapists, etc.

Like those non-empaths, you can use only your professional skill set at work, keeping your empath gift(s) turned OFF. Not only can you do that. It might even land you a raise. (See Gordon's story, coming soon.)

How about surviving childhood abuse, alcoholic parents, dysfunctional families, etc.? I see a lot of this pain second-hand in my RES sessions, as I help clients to release the STUFF they're still carrying from not-so-great childhoods.

(To learn about the many resources available in RES, in addition to the Empath Empowerment coaching, go to rose-rosetree.com and click on SESSIONS. You'll find dozens of energy spirituality skills that help folks to become more whole. And not one of them is "Do unskilled empath merges.")

If you feel stuck in any of the aforementioned buts, please consider: Having a couple of sessions with an RES expert might get you unstuck. Alternatively you also might simply do a bit of attitude adjustment and kick out those icky buts.

How Non-Empaths Cope

What will it mean, long term, to develop the habit of living with Space Dial at 1? Among my students, a new fear often creeps in around this stage in developing Empath Empowerment. If your Space Dial won't bring you big knowledge about everyone you meet, will you learn nothing about them at all?

Fear not. Becoming a skilled empath doesn't mean having your perceptiveness downgraded to the level of a charcoal briquette.

Allow me to introduce you to a very fine technique that you can use for getting information. Non-empaths use it and so can you.

You see, all caring people want to gather information about the people who matter to them. This urge to know can feel like an itch. In the past, as a not-yet-skilled empath, you would deal with this itch by doing innumerable unskilled empath merges. This was the equivalent of shooting an ant with a cannon but, hey, what did you know? Probably you didn't even know that you were an empath in the first place.

Back in the day you would often satisfy natural human curiosity by doing a quick, unskilled empath merge. Not by conscious decision but, rather, due to subconscious habit.

Please, give yourself a shout-out for being mega-talented. To you, doing that movement with consciousness was no big deal. Nonetheless, it was powerful. (Even if unskilled empath merge brought you Imported STUFF every single time, no exceptions.)

Non-empaths don't have that option. Yet, have you noticed? Somehow they manage to satisfy their human itch for inside information. They know about a technique that you have probably used on occasion, too. But now let's make it clear to your subconscious mind. What is this mysterious technique, and what can make it at least as powerful as doing unskilled empath merges?

Asking Human Questions

This is a very human technique, and so useful that it can help you way more than doing an unskilled empath merge.

Maybe you're wondering, what about Skilled Empath Merge? After you've learned that, can you go back to using it every day, off and on, all day long? Nope. Even if you go all the way through my series of Empath Empowerment books — proceeding from this Book 1 all the way through to Book 4, *The Master Empath*, you'll likely be very sparing in your use of Skilled Empath Merge.

Although a thrill to do, and very useful, doing Skilled Empath Merge is profoundly **spiritual**.

Whereas "Asking Human Questions" serves you better in everyday life. Simply because, skilled empath or not, you're definitely **human**.

Thus, accepting your humanity helps to empower you as an empath.

How do you use this amazing technique? Let's go step by step into how to succeed at Asking Human Questions.

- When you feel that familiar itch to get more information about somebody, create a question.
- Phrase it in plain, old everyday human language. This doesn't have to be highly sophisticated. Just make it a real question, rather than a generic, like "How ya doing?" or "Wassup?"
- The simple act of finding a question can help you to calm down and not feel inwardly pressured to use your empath superpowers.

Then what you do next can be very simple indeed:

1. **Ask your question out loud.**
2. **Listen to the answer.**
3. **Ask follow-up questions as needed.**

Hey, good (human) job!

Which Human Questions Are NOT Smart to Ask

Here come examples of questions that would not be especially smart to ask:

- After that 12-course banquet I just served you, are you still hungry?
- Why are you so mean?
- Are you mad at me or just perpetually cranky?
- Have I groveled enough to satisfy you for today?

Okay, maybe you wouldn't use exactly these words. Not out loud. Not directly to your significant other.

Merely deciding which questions you'd like to ask — Aha! That can bring you plenty of answers. Which sort of information do you want to know? Hmmmm.

It's perfectly safe to ask any question out loud... when alone in the bathroom. Otherwise, use some discernment before you ask you any random question to your significant other. Is that question really such a prize pony? Might it be more like a wounded cockroach?

Besides, your question may have a simple answer that you can figure out all by yourself, such as:

- Hello, Vinnie's in a bad mood.
- Vinnie's always in a bad mood.

Which might lead to more Asking Human Questions, like...

- Why on earth do I keep dating Vinnie? (Answer: Who cares? Time to break up with him already!)

Alternatives to Asking Human Questions

Maybe it isn't really so important that you seek deep knowledge of others, whether through our shiny new technique or by using your former fave, unskilled empath merge.

Instead you could learn all you need about people, for practical purposes, by simply paying attention to what these folks say and do.

You know, in regular human reality!

Another alternative is that you can use Your Formula for Better Communication, which you learned back on Day 17.

Different. But You Can Manage this Shift

Asking Human Questions, or the equivalent, can be quite a contrast to how you've been relating to other people. As the truth of what you've been doing becomes clear to you, you might go through some upset feelings. Sometimes becoming a skilled empath brings up issues and tissues.

If this happens, you don't have to hide it from your significant other. By now you're on Day 21 of a 30-Day Plan. Which you're hardly required to keep a secret.

Depending on the amount of suffering in your past, you may feel delicate about developing the social skill called "Asking Human Questions." Maybe you're worried about putting your best friend on the defensive. Then you can preface your questions briefly before asking them. Examples follow.

1. This may just be my fear, okay. But are you angry at me for breathing through my nose?
2. I've been worrying. When I do the laundry and our towels come out of the dryer only two-inches fluffy-soft, do you despise me as a person?
3. This may be a silly question. But when you come home, you never fold me in a big bear hug and tickle my toes. Of course, everybody knows that if you really, truly love someone, you do that daily. So I'm wondering, why haven't you ever tickled my toes?

Alas, there's a finite limit to how many questions like these I can supply for you. You're going to have to find the most important and personal ones on your own. Likewise, if you have resistance keeping your Space Dial at 1 in everyday life, only one person can find the solution, a person you know rather intimately.

But there is one more way I can help: Providing success stories. The following tales come from students who gained Empath Empowerment, even though it felt weird to them at first, keeping their Space Dials at 1. Maybe their stories will inspire you.

Juanita's Friendly Skies

When Juanita worked as a flight attendant, she attracted all the crazies. Mysterious but true....

There she would be, standing next to all her fellow crew members at the entrance to the plane, welcoming passengers. At first glance, Juanita could tell who would be trouble. Sure enough, during the flight they would ask for *her*, never the other flight attendants. The entire flight, troubled travelers would spill their sob stories, their insecurities, their multiple cocktails.

Nutty passengers would get out of their seats, walk down the aisles of the plane, and target Juanita. Then they would supply way too much information about their lives.

Juanita began to wonder if, unintentionally, she wore some kind of wacko-magnet on her airline uniform.

Actually, She Did.

Only that wacko-magnet was showing just in her aura. This magnet read:

"Space Dial turned up to 10. Ladies and gentlemen, get your free unskilled empath merge. Hurry, hurry, step right up. Dump your STUFF right here."

In practical terms, Juanita's aura wasn't terribly different from these famous words:

> *Give me your tired, your poor,*
> *Your huddled masses yearning to breathe free,*
> *The wretched refuse of your teeming shore.*
> *Send these, the homeless, tempest-tost to me.*

Sure, this is a great offer. Especially when given for free. However, this offer is appropriate for the Statue of Liberty, not a person made of flesh and blood.

Eventually Juanita decided to try an experiment. She would turn her Space Dial down to 1 and do everything in her job description, nothing more. And, especially, no more volunteering energetic support to every passenger on the plane. Instead, Juanita decided, her goals would be having a pleasant, easy flight (Priority #1) and doing her job (Priority #2).

In short, she'd just go through the motions.

Wowee! Crazies started heckling the other flight attendants. Crazies left Juanita alone. Incidentally, she kept her job, too.

Feeling better as a skilled empath, Juanita still used professional skills to help her passengers. Skills that had nothing to do with being an empath.

It's true. Space Dial at 10 is never, ever in your job description. Don't confuse volunteer work with a 9-5 job. And, speaking of jobs...

Gordon's Improved Performance Evaluation

Gordon had a problem with his boss. Mr. Boss was always telling Gordon, "You're too much." Yet Gordon had no clue what he was doing wrong, nor how he could stop being "too much."

From the way he described things to me, Gordon was an exemplary employee. Yet he also happened to be an unskilled empath, which meant that he was constantly doing unskilled empath merges.

After studying with me, Gordon developed the habit of keeping his empath gifts OFF. (Other than when doing Skilled Empath Merges, on purpose, and in moderation.)

Returning to work, Gordon automatically kept his Space Dial at 1 whenever he dealt with Mr. Boss.

Soon Mr. Boss was telling him, "I don't know why but lately I've started feeling more comfortable with you."

Mr. Boss started taking Gordon out to lunch. Instead of being fired, Gordon received a promotion.

What Made the Difference?

When you keep your empath gift(s) ON constantly, the recipient of your attention will notice. In a way.

Mr. Boss doesn't have to be an empath in order to tell that something is happening on the level of consciousness. It can be just a vague feeling.

Moreover, Mr. Boss may never tell you his reaction in words. Consciously he may never notice a thing. Nonetheless, he'll react subconsciously.

Could your empath skills win you more money and prestige at work? Well, it's happened to many of my clients and students. Why not you?

Your Assignment for Day 21

Brave Explorer, here's your job for today:

1. If you want to learn more about people, use your words, not your empath gift(s). When you have questions, try Asking Human Questions rather than relying on your familiar method of finding answers through unskilled empath merges.
2. Lavish attention on the objective side of relationships, rather than your subjective commentaries. (Ironically, this may make you *more* popular.)
3. After you turn your empath gift(s) OFF, what if you start feeling guilt or some other discomfort? Notice that. Then repeat this helpful phrase, "So what?" Emphasize whatever else is interesting as you go your merry way, being The Most Important Person in the Room.

DAY 22

New Eyes

Thanks to The Furniture Game and Asking Human Questions, you're gaining control over how you hold a space with others. Yesterday should have helped, too. But maybe you're grumbling like Jocelyn, who still is fixated on eyes:

"Sorry, Rose, but I've simply got to look everyone in the eye. Otherwise, I feel inauthentic. Turning off empath gifts is fine. But where's the fun in life if you can't look at people's eyes all you want?"

Gee, would I be capable of understanding that? As a lovelorn teenager, I taped just one crush-worthy picture on my bedroom walls. Actually, I placed it on the ceiling, right above my bed. It was two pages from an art book, two super-enlarged photographs of Pablo Picasso's eyes. One page per eye. My centerfold.

Yes, I kept those humungous eyes above my bed so that I could stare at them meaningfully. This brought much-needed variety to my hours of insomnia.

Jocelyn, and everyone else, I know better than to demand that you permanently forego looking at eyes all you want. I'm only warning you: If you were born as an empath, no matter which gift(s) you have, guess what happens as soon as you look directly at any live person's eyes for two seconds straight?

Your consciousness starts to travel into that person's aura. If you are not a very, extremely, hugely accomplished skilled empath, you'll do a quick unskilled empath merge and take some of that person's STUFF directly into your aura.

The exceptions would be if you're watching a photo or screen image. Or you're staring at your *own* eyes for two seconds or more for a practical purpose, such as inserting contact lenses or applying eye makeup. In this case, you're treating yourself like furniture, right?

During our 30 Days, you're experimenting, and with something far more interesting than plum-colored eyeliner. I'm helping you to land squarely into your own life, saving empath merges for special occasions.

My purpose isn't to deprive you of adventure but to help you to discover one great big adventure: Being yourself, through and through, whether with friends or not, always and consistently remaining The Most Important Person in The Room.

Come to think of it, haven't you started to feel differently about yourself since your Day 1 with this book? Yes? No? Either way, here's a fun idea.

Skill Sneaking up on Me. A Quiz

It's quiz time, Brave Explorer. Please answer YES, NO, or MAYBE to each of the following questions.

1. I *am* becoming more aware of myself, my full set of mind-body-spirit-intellect-soul-emotions-environment.
2. I have started to have fun with these different aspects of myself, choosing to jump into different categories rather than mostly staying stuck at one of them.
3. At least once during the last three days, I have purposely pulled awareness away from emotions or intellect or spirit, thinking something like, "There can be more to my life than this." Then I have chosen to direct my consciousness elsewhere, to another part of my personal Bingo card... and it worked.
4. When I'm in the room with other people, I have been paying more attention to myself than before.

5. God hasn't struck me dead for doing this. In fact, nobody has been injured by the subtle, personal choice to shift my consciousness back to myself.
6. I'm actually beginning to grow comfortable with the idea of treating myself like The Most Important Person in The Room. It has stopped seeming so selfish and started feeling perfectly reasonable.
7. I have noticed that other people in my life, the non-empaths, really do have their Space Dials turned down to 1 most of the time. This doesn't make them monsters. They're just very focused on their own lives.
8. Also, I've started noticing how some people (especially empaths) stick to other people like glue. There's a possible smothering effect on the person being stuck to. In the past, I didn't notice this, but now I do: *The recipient of an unskilled empath's attention doesn't necessarily like it.*
9. My amount of worrying has gone way down, come to think of it
10. Subtly, it has become easier to keep my mind on work. I'm getting more accomplished by just being me — without adding all that volunteer work.
11. Although I continue to use The Wakeup Call as needed to clear out STUFF from others, I'm not having to do it as often. Could I be clearer than before? Could I get used to feeling more powerful, more like myself?

For every YES answer, congratulate yourself. MAYBE's aren't bad, either. You're becoming a skilled empath at your own pace, that's all.

Now you win a prize for taking that Skill Quiz. Something new to learn. Woo-hoo!

Who Owns Your Eyes, Anyway?

Did you know? There's one easy way to pick unskilled empaths out of a crowd.

Just watch how they use their eyes. Many unskilled empaths stare like babies. (The exception to this rule is the mating behavior of non-empaths and empaths alike. When love-struck, all people do an awful lot of staring.)(And, of course, another exception is the stoner eyes of folks when on weed.)

But Now, Let's Think about You!

Before you began our 30-Day Plan, didn't you tend to stare at people, especially looking them straight in the eye? Would you like to have *more* (not *fewer*) ways of using your eyes, and do it risk free? Today we're going to explore new techniques that, besides being fun, will add to your skill as an empath.

In the past you had just one major choice about how you used your eyes in social situations. Would you stare, yes or no? But you've already learned some useful alternatives:

- With The Furniture Game, you explored a new choice that combined intention ("like furniture") with the use of your own personal eyeballs.
- With Eye Option #1, you stopped automatically making eye contact for social reasons. Instead, you experimented with looking *near* eyes, not *at* them.
- With Eye Option #2, you were invited to experiment by taking only *a quick glance,* one second or less, rather than jumping in for a prolonged stare.

Thus, you have started to gain control over how you use your eyes. Which leaves you feeling better than before. Which is the point.

Except What If Some of You Have Been Cheating?

'Fess up, have you been doing all the other techniques in our 30-Day Plan, just not this one? So you didn't want to make the sacrifice!

Well, that's akin to a dieter who eats sensibly all day long except, at night, he or she absolutely must devour that big carton of ice cream.

If you have been cheating with your eyes, think about this: Who do those eyes belong to, anyway? Maybe somebody else expects to enjoy that momentary soothing feeling right after your unskilled empath merges, even though that person's pain comes back soon afterwards. Plus, of course, you're the one who'll be left dealing with Imported STUFF. To make a technical assessment, "Phooey on that-ey."

If Roscoe needs that kind of help, trust me. He'll be able to find it. You're not the only empath with eyeballs. In America, 1 out of 20 people is an empath and most of them probably do have eyeballs.

Let somebody else volunteer. In the unlikely event that Roscoe can't find another unskilled empath, maybe he'll hit bottom and start taking responsibility for solving his own problems.

Resolve to Do No Harm. With Your Eyes

Managing the use of your eyeballs, imagine! Brave Explorer, you can live like a doctor who takes the Hippocratic Oath. From now on, do no harm, not to people like Roscoe (by enabling them) and not to yourself, either.

You can actually use your eyes to make yourself The Most Important Person in The Room. There's a whole set of techniques for this. I call them "Eye Muscles."

Unlike my old Picasso eyes on the ceiling, live people have muscles for moving their eyes. Although eyes can move quite nicely with *involuntary* muscles, eyes can also be moved by means of *voluntary* muscles. It's like breathing, which normally goes by itself. But you might consciously change how you breathe for yoga or acting or singing or spitting.

Voluntary control of your eyes is essential for Empath Empowerment. Yet unskilled empaths seldom take control. Instead, they indulge in a trusting kind of stare that brings on unskilled empath merges.

Suppose that James, still an unskilled empath, is in a room when Lexi enters. All the time they're together, James looks at her as if she's the star of his movie.

Poor besotted James. (You already know about his hopeless crush, right?) Often James makes matters worse for himself by prolonged staring at Lexi's eyes. Whenever James does this, his consciousness does super-fast unskilled Empath Merges with Lexi, taking on more of her STUFF. Which could help explain why, at the end of the day, James feels as though he belongs in a recycle bin.

Yecch!

Eye Muscles

This techniques helps you to live as the star of your own movie.

Decide how far to move out with your eyes. Those eyes do belong to you, correct?

Here is a set of five advanced eye techniques for empaths. Used them alone or in sequence, as desired.

1. Look in the *very near distance.* Move your vision out just a little, eyes angled downward, aiming very close to you, only a few feet ahead.
2. Look out *mid-range.* You're moving eyes farther away this time. Don't aim really far from you but at a comfortable middle distance.
3. Look *very far out* now, as if aiming for the horizon. To do this, move your eyes so the gaze lifts upward.
4. Activate your *sideways* eye muscles. Slowly alternate moving your eyes to the left, then center-ish, then to the right. Moving sideways, you can choose whether to look mid-range or up close. You might even notice objects

with your peripheral vision, out the corner of one eye. Are your eyes clever or what?

5. When you're in the room with somebody else, choose not to focus constantly on that person. Who are you going to make The Most Important Person in The Room? It's you, with those fine eye muscles. So alternate:

- Sometimes looking at other people
- Sometimes looking elsewhere

That's right. No longer must you automatically focus 100% on other people in the room. Your eyes obey YOU.

Maybe You're Wondering

But are these eye tricks socially acceptable? Sure, provided you don't dart your eyes around super-fast or roll them around like pinwheels.

Every time you make a voluntary shift to eye position, you're using your own consciousness to control which person in the room becomes the most important to you.

Aim your eyes purposely and the very act of choosing makes you The Most Important Person in The Room.

Incidentally, if you're shy about trying out this new eye behavior in front of people you know, practice while watching TV.

Drag your eyes away from the actor who is speaking lines and notice how other actors react. Or check out the furniture, on-screen or off-screen.

Golly will the actors' show still go on? Find out.

Hypnotism Alert

Hypnotists aren't the only ones who put people into trances, you know.

People put themselves into trances. James, for instance, puts himself into a trance by staring at Lexi.

Being an unskilled empath means often putting yourself into an unskilled empath's trance, one where you (Sob!) never get to be The Most Important Person in The Room.

It's human to identify with others. Most people do it most of the time. But if you're an empath, you don't simply identify with somebody like Lexi. Your empath gift(s) turn ON and, before you know it, that Space Dial twirls up to a 10.

Letting this happen is optional for you now. This skill comes none too soon, because every unskilled empath trance brings consequences. And these may not be terribly good for you. Here are three example of unskilled empath merge being seriously dangerous, once upon a time. But these workshop students quickly learned to develop skills anyway. (If they can do it, you sure can!)

Brad's Trance of Misery

Once I gave a workshop where the graduate, Brad, told this story:

"I began noticing the problem in second grade. Pain from the other kids would come into me and I didn't know how to stop it. Now I know I'm an empath with the gift of Physical Oneness.

"Before, all I knew was that I would develop health problems 'for no reason.' Altogether I was hospitalized 12 times because of different health problems that really came from other people. I knew what was happening, only I was powerless to stop it.

"Studying with you has been the first time I can remember when I could be in a room with other people and pay attention to myself."

Musical Chairs with Maxi

Maxi, another student in that workshop, told her story of life in an unskilled empath's trance.

"Now I know that I have Emotional Oneness, Emotional Intuition, Spiritual Oneness, Spiritual Intuition, and also Physical Oneness. Before, I knew only this: Whenever I was with other people, I would take on their anger, their worries and even their aches and pains.

"Whenever I would ride the subway, sitting next to a stranger, I would take on her problems. After I couldn't stand it any more, I would change seats. Sometimes I would use up every seat in that subway car. Then I would have to move to another subway car and start changing seats all over again.

"That's how it was until yesterday, Day One of our workshop. But when I came here today for Day Two of our workshop, I didn't have to change seats once. I just realized that now."

Towanda's Transport

Towanda, another woman in that same workshop, decided to tell her story, too.

"I used to change seats, too. Not as many as Maxi. But I sure took on problems. Then I'd get so overwhelmed, I would throw up. I'm really curious what life will be like for me now. Welcome to the world of not throwing up!"

Maybe your unskilled empath trance states haven't been so extreme. Even if you suffered just a smidge before, you need not suffer even that much. Because you've learned so many ways to wake up from an unskilled empath's trance and take charge of your life.

Break the Spell

Now let's add one more technique to your skill set. Use our Break the Spell technique any time you're awake, unless driving a car or operating other potentially dangerous machinery.

Whenever you start to feel that you are turning your Space Dial higher because of someone else in the room, tear your eyes away. Look at yourself. It could be a wrist, an ankle, a piece of clothing, the color of the skin on your hand, etc.

Of course, you won't look at *yourself* like a piece of furniture, right? Be interested in that chosen fragment of self. Looking at yourself, even your clothes, begin the connection. Intensify it by asking questions like these:

- How do I feel emotionally right now. (Just one quick little answer please, not depth analysis.)
- Am I moving or still?
- How does my body feel physically? (Choose one small part to explore at a time, like one elbow or toe.)

Anything you notice about yourself will do quite nicely to Break the Spell. Just being in the room with someone else does not mean you need slip into a hypnotic trance where that other person becomes your main reality.

You never need to identify with another person unless you choose to, nor need you twirl your Space Dial all the way up to 10. Because your life *is* all about you. At least it can be.

Break the Spell whenever you wish. Afterwards, when you're good and ready, go back to looking at other people in the room. They can handle your momentary lack of attention.

Actually, unless they're babies, they can handle your *long-term* lack of attention. Apart from youngsters in your care, other people seldom need your full attention. Why? They give it to themselves.

Your Assignment for Day 22

Can you emphasis your experience and thoughts and needs while with others? Sure you can.

And now you know, how you move your eyes can help. So today, experiment at will with our shiny new techniques, Break the Spell and Eye Muscles.

By doing this assignment, Brave Explorer, guess what? You'll complete Part Two of your training for Empath Empowerment.

A Skilled Empath Among Friends

PART THREE

The Fun of Being a Skilled Empath

As a skilled empath, you become an *equal* member of the crowd. Using your skills to help others, you remain free of their pain. And you can be yourself fully. Easily. Always.

By now, you have explored many ways to be yourself, regardless of who's in the room along with you. Keeping your empath gift(s) OFF isn't done by stiffening your boundaries or any other quick gimmick. Instead, you've developed a skill set for using your consciousness. Don't you find it quite easy now, holding a space for yourself as The Most Important Person in The Room?

In ways that you wouldn't have been able to understand back at Day 1, you have so many choices. They include mind-body-spirit-intellect-soul-emotions-environment, plus how you can direct consciousness through your eyes. No more unskilled empath merges for you!

So what's left to learn? In Part Three of our 30-Day Plan, you'll add exciting new skills and have even more fun. Gain the full benefit of my experience, coaching thousands of empaths like you. I don't merely want you to suffer *less*. I want you to enjoy *more*.

As you refine your skills at Empath Empowerment, each day can bring new discoveries. Soon you will access techniques that safely turn your empath gift(s) ON all the way, Space Dial safely set at 10.

Resulting in how much Imported STUFF?

None.

How come? Because you're doing a technique designed to provide maximum insight along with zero unskilled merging whatsoever.

It will be my delight, teaching you how to do a Skilled Empath Merge. Frankly, it's the biggest fun you can have with your clothes on.

DAY 23

Body Language Turned Inside Out

Let's summarize your current skill set as you enter Part Three of our 30-Day Plan for Empath Empowerment. Haven't you made awesome progress at keeping your empath gift(s) turned OFF in most social situations?

Doing this will become increasingly comfortable with practice. Realistically, our plan takes 30 days, not 30 hours. But at least paying attention to yourself from the inside is growing easier, right? All the following skills can help:

- *Paying attention to yourself* has become a more vivid and fascinating experience. In the past, maybe you were mostly alive in just one aspect of yourself, like emotions, but now you have begun to explore the full range of your very distinctive human personality: Mind-body-spirit-intellect-soul-emotions-environment. **MBS. I See!**

- Whenever you're ready for *personal growth,* you can repeat techniques from Mind Day, Body Day, etc. This will help more neglected aspects of yourself to come fully alive.

- You know how to use your awareness to keep *evolving in a balanced way.* For continued progress, you have techniques like the Be Deep Quickie and Inner Bingo.

- Based on familiarity with your inner resources, you have learned to *experiment with how you hold a space.* Most intensely, The Furniture Game helps your aura stay put, so you don't bounce in and out of unskilled empath merges.

Even a few minutes of The Furniture Game can reposition your consciousness, giving you an hour or more with your Space Dial turned to 1.

Admittedly, keeping your Space Dial that low could still feel weird for a few more days or weeks. Soon it won't. As an empath, remember this practical equation:

My empath gift(s) turned OFF =

Being The Most Important Person in The Room

Soon you won't need to cheerlead yourself to do this, muttering encouraging words to yourself, like "Furniture."

Worried?

Despite my reassurance, some of you Brave Explorers still may be worrying. "What if moving that Space Dial down makes me feel guilty?"

Remember, Space Dial turned to 1 is how non-empaths live most of the time. (And that doesn't make them narcissists.) Eventually, you will actually *enjoy* keeping your Space Dial at 1 most of the time. Doing so will prod you to find human-level ways to connect to others, ways that do not involve using your deepest qualities of consciousness.

Actions don't merely speak louder than words. They can take less out of you. Here's a snapshot of everyday life for a skilled empath:

1. **When you're with others, you habitually focus on *objective* reality, seeing people and events more clearly than unskilled empaths do.**
2. **Since you're an empath, a rich and fascinating *subjective* reality will await you whenever you make a shift inward.**
3. **But here's the new part about your subjective reality *now.* That rich inner life doesn't require turning ON your gift(s) as an empath. You're starting to sort things out properly. An empath's gifts are meant for experiencing**

what it is like to be *other* people, and this is no substitute for paying attention to yourself as a regular human being.
4. Interacting with people as a skilled empath, you honor yourself and advocate for yourself, acting as though your life matters. Sure, sometimes you'll become curious about other people, like "What's with Troy and his announcement that I must watch him practice for his big audition as Macbeth?"
5. But you will balance curiosity about others by giving yourself equal time. For instance, you might follow up your question about Troy with, "And what interests me now about me? What's going on in *my* mind-body-spirit-intellect-soul-emotions-environment?"

As you grow increasingly comfortable with the position of Space Dial at 1, you'll find that some of that adventurous feeling you used to get by doing unskilled empath merges with others… the very best of that freedom and exhilaration… can be generated at will by switching from one part of your subjective reality to another.

It's a big deal that you have all seven (Count 'em, 7!!!!!!!) inner playgrounds: Mind + body + spirit + intellect + soul + emotions + way of being in the environment. Moving from one to another, at will, has become your standard skill set. It's like your daily bread-and-butter.

Now Add Jelly

As they say in the infomercials, "And there's more."

Today I want to give you a hilarious new way to turn that Space Dial to 1. Variety is sweet, like adding jelly to your bread and butter.

Really, it's perfectly reasonable for us empaths to crave outer variety nearly as much as we crave inner stability.

One man's deep is another man's shallow.

This "ancient proverb" — okay, I just made it up now — means that some things in life, which usually are considered a big deal, might actually be quite puny. The difference depends on whether you're a non-empath or an empath.

Remember the wild idea, stated near the beginning of this book, that becoming a skilled empath can turn your reality inside out? If you're an empath, many things in life are the exact opposite of what you've been told.

Body language gives us a perfect example of the inside-out shift that's involved, going from clueless empath to skilled empath.

Body Language for a Non-Empath

BODY LANGUAGE means studying nonverbal communication to learn more about what's going on with a person. Body language is often considered a big deal. And it is… for a non-empath. Consider our pal Troy.

- Normally, his consciousness is locked up in the four walls of his body. Other people seem like a baffling mystery.
- Even though he's used to being The Most Important Person in The Room, Troy has decided he would like to learn more about other people.
- For a non-empath like him, studying body language can help a lot. Troy can learn about people's insides from their outsides.
- To Troy, other people may never seem fully important, not compared to him. At least body language can help him understand them a bit better.
- So Troy starts noticing items of body language, then interpreting what he sees. For him, this new knowledge will count as way deep.

But how deep is body language for you, as a born empath? Let's make a comparison. The only tricky part of this is how, in the past, you may have done extra when reading body language. Your version could really have been a more-or-less conscious unskilled empath merge.

Strictly speaking, body language involves paying attention to one item of facial expression or body posture at a time. Then you interpret what shows on the surface.

Sometimes an empath will learn about body language and use that as a springboard, much as psychics can start doing Tarot readings and transition from that into full-blown psychic readings that don't use cards at all.

So when we considering what body language means for an empath, remember that we're referring to body language alone, nothing extra.

Body Language for an EMPATH

What can the study of body language offer an empath like you?

Normally, your consciousness travels in and out of other people. *Locating your own self* has been the baffling mystery.

Now you're learning to use your gift(s) on purpose, becoming The Most Important Person in The Room. Still, you long to learn more about the inner lives of people like Troy. If only there could be a way to do this and keep your Space Dial at 1.

Hooray, there is such a way! It's studying body language. This kind of perception begins by focusing on someone like Troy's physical appearance.

How refreshing is that? You're not noticing how he feels inside his mind-body-spirit-intellect-soul-emotions-environment but simply how he moves that obvious, outermost physical self.

Body language helps you to gain information about Troy from a comfortable distance, while keeping your Space Dial at 1.

To you, this new knowledge is refreshingly shallow, perfect for entertaining yourself while you keep your empath gift(s) turned OFF.

Seriously!

Think I'm kidding that body language is mostly used as something deep for non-empaths? Check out workshops and books on body language. Non-empaths can get so excited, you'd think they had found the Holy Grail.

Sales pitches for body language emphasize how the knowledge will help you to control people so you can sell them things, earn yourself money, etc. Not necessarily an empath's typical motivatin for learning what it's like to be another person!

People become so excited because they can finally tell *something* — anything — about what happens to others on the inside. All that glee makes sense, given what you know now about people used to being The Most Important Person in The Room. But will funny old body language bring anyone a really deep experience of Otherness?

Yes, Otherness

OTHERNESS means the direct experience of someone or something else like a crystal or plant. Instead of emphasizing your distinctive versions of mind-body-spirit-intellect-soul-emotions-environment.

And instead of having your usual habits of relying on some of these categories more than others! With Otherness you move into a different way of having consciousness.

Because every person, plant, animal, crystal, machine, and earth environment does have its own distinctive consciousness. To experience Otherness, a non-empath would need to study aura reading. Then Otherness come in the form of information. (By contrast, for an empath who reads auras, Otherness comes as a direct, personal experience.) Body language won't really give a non-empath knowledge of Otherness. Instead, there's information at a superficial level. At least, observing body language can move a non-empath in a deeper direction.

The Body Language Game

Now that you're oriented, here how to play with our latest technique for Empath Empowerment. Whenever you start to notice a person's body language, remember that physical bodies are perceived at the surface of life.

So the act of noticing body positions and expression will shift your consciousness up to the surface of reality. Automatic positioning causes your Space Dial will re-set at 1.

1. Notice one specific item at a time. (Examples will follow.) Aim to stay on the surface, reading expression and body position.
2. Figure out the meaning of your specific item. Develop your own system. Or, if you've been reading a body language book with someone else's system, consider if the suggested interpretation seems true to you. Evaluating in that way can help to fine-tune your interpretations.
3. With no effort required, your Space Dial will re-set at 1.

In honor of you, Brave Explorers and my fellow empaths, here's information adapted from one of my books about deeper perception, *Read People Deeper*.

Hand Insights

Here are those examples I promised you earlier, simple yet interesting things you can notice about body language.

- ∽ Observe how your partner moves hands while talking. Are they flexible, stiff, forceful, sensitive, creative, responsive? (Yes, hands can definitely be considered phallic symbols.)

- A partner who prizes sensuousness will show it in *grooming,* especially of hands. They're vital sensual tools. So it's revealing to see if they're either showcased or neglected. How much care has gone into the nails? Have those hands been kept clean?
- *Touch quality,* from those very same hands, is another tip-off to sensuousness. How does your partner handle objects? Watch him/her pick up car keys or hold a glass of water.
- Do sparks fly when your partner's fingers make contact with your body? Be it a handshake, a shoulder pat, or a caress of your cheek, some hands shine like spotlights for *physical intelligence.*
- Other kinds of sensuality show that a person is *awake intuitively.* Does your partner's hand seem to read your emotions, your energy, your sexual interest, how you feel physically?

Your Assignment for Day 23

Your highly entertaining assignment for today is to purposely play the Body Language Game.

Read other people, right on the surface. Do this at least three times. Before and after, notice how you feel. Don't you remain yourself, STUFF-free?

Brave Explorer, I hope you'll remember. One quick reading of body language is enough to twirl your Space Dial back to 1. If you were born as an empath, that is what body language does best.

DAY 24

First-Date Somebody Wonderful

Married? Single? Leading a double life, or a triple one? Regardless, today's assignment can suit you just fine. Keep your lifestyle. Just start dating somebody new.

For the adventurous, dating always opens up interesting possibilities. Haven't you heard amazing stories about first dates? Here's one that I heard.

Melvin as Soul Mate

"Melvin and I met for drinks after work. Then we went back to my place to talk. We talked. We made love. We talked more, until 3:00 in the morning.

"After we woke up, we started talking again. It was so wonderful, we could hardly tear ourselves away to go to work. That's how it has been between us ever since. Melvin is my soul mate."

Well, here's a contrasting tale about dating. Susie and John are entering a party. They've been together a very long time and are making their game plan for this event.

Planning for a Most Unromantic Visit

JOHN: "Why should I bother with talking to you at this party? Much as I love you, let's admit it. We already know everything about each other."

"The whole point of a party is the new blood. I'm going to join the conversation over there, and don't you dare follow me. Find your own people."

SUSIE: "I couldn't agree more. Leave me alone while I explore what makes these people tick. I've got to. Staying with you, I could die of boredom."

Guess what? A version of Susie and John's conversation probably occurs regularly within your own subconscious mind. Empaths can treat *themselves* like a long-suffering spouse, so very taken for granted.

Pal, How Do You Talk to Yourself?

Look, you have been making great progress at turning your empath gift(s) OFF. You're having thrilling conversations. You have carried out *Melvin as Soul Mate*-like encounters with your own mind-body-spirit-intellect-soul-emotions-environment.

Altogether, you're more than halfway there, falling in love with yourself as The Most Important Person in The Room.

But sometimes doesn't it still feel empty, paying so much attention to yourself? As if life without constant empathic travel into other people's auras could make you boring!

Well, you're never really boring, not for a minute. But how you treat yourself as a person… that could definitely be boring.

Consider this possibility. You might be due for a self-dating upgrade. How do you treat yourself in your spare time? Whenever you find yourself even slightly bored with yourself today, you can actively start to first-date yourself. Here's what I mean.

Yes, You Can First-Date Yourself

Why wait for Mr. Right or Ms. Right to suddenly materialize to do the job for you. No more searching for Melvin! Instead, act interested in yourself.

Ask yourself questions out loud, the kind you would ask on a good first date.

Following that, respond enthusiastically. Also, out loud. Then keep the conversational ball rolling.

For instance:

A. "Looking around where we are right now, what looks really good to you? "

B. You're right, that *is* beautiful.

A. Do you like sports? What do you think of those Mets?

B. Interesting! Your perspective is so refreshing. Now, I've heard you also have quite the brain for politics. What do you think is the most important issue in our country today?

Responses matter when first dating yourself. And, yes, this is to be a non-stop conversation, as with somebody new who is absolutely fascinating.

Assume that you want to know all about this promising new date. Ask plenty of questions. And don't be shy about revealing yourself. Put all your feelings into words. Scatter opinions liberally, just like your praise:

- Clever! Outrageous!
- Aw, you're so witty. What a great thing you just said!

Silly?

Sure, I'll admit that. First-dating yourself may seem outrageously silly. You might even be talking aloud to yourself more than normal.

However, if you're even moderately observant, you'll notice that plenty of other people talk to themselves, too. And they're not having nearly as good a time.

Why? They're just mumbling to self like a burned-out old spouse. You, by contrast, are on a fabulous first date.

Dating Happens Often. In Consciousness

Because we're talking about a *successful* first date, naturally. Dating yourself today, the intent isn't to practice your sneer.

A winning first date includes sincere curiosity. You're curious and respectful, more apt to praise than to blame.

Frankly, unskilled empaths can act more like promiscuous, frantic daters of any random stranger in the room. Say that James is at a Seven Eleven. It's located far away from home. Waiting in line, he notices Wilhelmina, someone he'll never see again, let alone date.

Yet standing in line to buy his Diet Coke, unbeknownst to his conscious mind, James might do his usual unskilled empath merging version of "dating."

1. Hey, Wilhelmina, what's it like to be you?
2. How do you feel emotionally, Wilhelmina, my new buddy?
3. Can I send you some energy?
4. Long as I'm popping in and out of your aura, why don't I take on some of your pain?
5. No need to thank me.
6. Waiting in line, I'll casually monitor your thinking process. Nice job.

Or sometimes an unskilled empath like James will stand in line and lament that he *doesn't* have a date with Wilhelmina (or anyone else).

1. Here I am stuck in line at this pathetic Seven Eleven.
2. Alone again. If only I were on a date, it wouldn't be so bad. We'd have fun. Even here, we'd manage to have fun somehow.

3. Will I always be alone?
4. Where, oh where, is my soul mate?

By Comparison, First-Dating Yourself Isn't Half Bad

Never again need you be bored with your companion — since that companion is you. Never again need you treat yourself like an estranged spouse, so full of resentment that you could go out to dinner with S.O. and like each other so little, you eat in hostile silence.

If they choose, any couple can treat each other with first-date curiosity. Well, you can treat yourself that way, too.

Admittedly there are other cures for boredom. If you can't stand being alone with yourself, you might benefit from some professional help from the energy healer or therapist of your choice.

Or you might simply cover your naked body with sliced salami (for the variety). But my recommendation for today is the following technique. It's simple, cheap and relatively inconspicuous.

First-Dating on Your Big Night

Imagine, if it were Prom Night, or some other ultra-festive occasion, wouldn't you be on your best behavior?

Bring that attitude when you first-date yourself. Notice that person's adorable body, sparkling intellect, loving heart.

Compliments would be appreciated.

Get to know this amazing person further by asking loads of questions.

- What do you think of this place?
- Sure I'm interested. I *want* to know your opinion. Why do you have that reaction?
- Absolutely right! What else do you think?

Answer each question enthusiastically, even if it's just a running commentary while doing everyday errands.

And you know what's especially freeing about this kind of date? You can say all you want about ME-ME-ME and never risk seeming too interested in yourself!

First-date yourself a few times each day, seeing your life through fresh eyes. You'll build self-esteem and gratitude, appreciating what you've got going for you.

Whatever happened in your childhood, however much attention parents did or didn't give you, and regardless of the present state of your love life, you can make this first date excellent!

Have more of them tomorrow and then happily ever after.

Your Assignment for Day 24

Show interest in yourself as a person and first-date yourself. Do it at least twice today, each time for two minutes or longer.

If you want to be extra fancy, try the Be Deep Quickie both before and after.

Before you try this assignment, Brave Explorer, paying so much attention to yourself, out loud, may seem silly. But what might you discover? First-dating yourself could prove surprisingly helpful.

What if the relationship develops into a real love match? You just might wind up joyfully, powerfully aware of YOU, Space Dial set at 1.

DAY 25

Grounding or Jail

Being an Empowered Empath is not a weird lifestyle. Zachary's bathroom, with his surprising array of grooming products, now, that's a weird lifestyle. Empaths stay clear by subtle shifts of consciousness, not by using their own distinctive blend of hair spray and Miracle Gro.

As a skilled empath, you're invited to make subtle changes to your lifestyle. Even tiny changes, like the occasional First-Date Yourself, can make it easier to keep your empath gift(s) OFF most of the time.

Starting Day 28, this new lifestyle will become a basis for turning your empath gift(s) ON. It's your birthright to do Skilled Empath Merges as desired, and do them safely without taking on other people's STUFF. Soon, but not yet!

Meanwhile, *grounding* is today's term to sum up the Turn OFF part of that lifestyle. GROUNDING means inhabiting your body and the rest of your human life… as if it were real and you liked it.

Sex is not the only way this can happen. For almost every activity in life, you can choose a version that is grounding.

By contrast, turning empath gift(s) ON means *expanding spiritually*. Many other choices and habits cause expansion, like playing music, texting friends, eating sweets, drinking wine. They're pleasurable because expansion brings a high.

Nevertheless, expansion comes at a price. One way or another, you will need to integrate every bit of that expansion. If you don't do this voluntarily, life will do it to you. And it won't be pretty.

Remember before you started our 30-Day Plan? If you're like most of my students, you had the habit of expanding so often with unskilled empath merges, you couldn't comfortably keep up with the integrating part.

Whooshing in and out of others with your aura may feel like "me," but it's really a matter of lifestyle, a habit. Alas, the habit of "not being in your surroundings or body" can come back to bite you.

Drama Vs. Gentler Invitations

Huge weight gain, inability to stop smoking, chronic pain, poverty, Zachary's reluctance to shampoo — problems like these can be pretty dramatic warnings about being ungrounded.

Think of stories you've heard where drama was blamed on bad luck: So-called "accidents," getting fired for "no reason," health problems that come "out of nowhere." In seemingly random ways, someone you care about becomes a victim. Only maybe he or she isn't a victim so much as a person who didn't listen to life's gentler invitations.

Think about Zachary, going through a stage where he isn't grounded enough to function effectively in everyday life. Since he doesn't much value objective reality, how will he notice life's subtler hints that he's off balance? How can life let Zachary know when there is a problem?

That's one reason (not the only reason, but a surprisingly common one) why bad things happen to good people. Drama can be God's way of remaining anonymous.

Suppose that Zachary isn't in his body much, consciously. That body can't tap him on the shoulder and holler "Hellooooo" to grab his attention. Instead, he'll attract very attention-grabbing events from outside himself. (A.k.a. Drama).

Brave Explorer, accept life's kinder invitations. Develop the habit of paying attention to your body and environment, especially when unusual things happen around you. When your lifestyle balances expansion with plenty of grounding, you'll attract less drama.

Once you decide to pay attention to life's gentle invitations, you may notice more of them. Good!

For instance, say that you lock yourself out of the house. Again. Don't just stomp your feet angrily once you've managed to get back inside your own home. Consider yourself warned: More grounding may be needed.

Here's a personal example of an invitation to become more grounded. Once I managed to drop my wristwatch down the kitchen sink.

Not only did this ruin my device for measuring human time. Since I was too spaced out to notice when or where the watch slid off my wrist, later I had to bring in a repairman to fix the garbage disposal.

Turns out, garbage disposals don't like to chew up wristwatches. Throwing human timekeeping device in the garbage? Nice symbolic touch! It was a pretty strong invitation to ground myself more.

Maybe you're wondering, what difference can it make if you do start to notice your invitations?

A ridiculously big difference!

When it comes to an invitation to live more grounded, you can win. Just add something extra for grounding. You can become a person who sprinkles plenty of delicious bits of grounding into each day. Here's a list of choices, in the form of a gentle quiz.

Which Choice Would Benefit You More?

Brave Explorer, for each of the following pairs of options, choose the one that seems smarter to you.

A. Meditate on your chakras, the energy of the universe, or transcending your body altogether.

B. Include time in your meditation to feel your physical body or to explore your connection to Mother Earth.

A. Arrive at appointments whenever you're in the mood.

B. Be — or become — punctual.

A. Spend money whenever you feel like it.

B. Stick to a budget.

A. Upon arising, go through your morning routine on autopilot, e.g., Barely notice your body until you have filled up at the coffee pump.

B. Use every part of your morning routine to re-establish your mind-body connection, e.g., When you brush your teeth, notice that you have teeth.

A. Check messages on your cell and your email more often than you notice your feet.

B. For every time that you turn on technology (laptop, mobile phone, etc.), give yourself 30 seconds to wiggle your toes.

A. So far, you have never learned how to relax your body on purpose.

B. Find some fun ways to intentionally relax your body, like stretching, blinking extra and then returning to normal. Yes, fun!

A. Breath is something to notice only if you're out of it.

B. At least once per hour, take a loooong, sloooow, breath.

A. If any food tempts you, it must be eaten. It's as though food can become The Most Important Person in The Room.

B. Occasionally ask your body "What would feel good to you right now?" Then do it.

(Incidentally, just because food happens to be near you doesn't make it more important than your own body's needs. Also, if it's still hard for you to be around certain ultra-tempting kinds of food, don't allow them in the place where you are.)

A. Your diet lavishly emphasizes uppers like sugar, white flour, and alcohol. But you're stingy with downers, like protein, complex carbs, and oils.

B. Your diet emphasizes grounders like protein, complex carbs, and oils. Your diet is stingy with trippy foods like sugar, simple carbs, and alcohol.

A. Generally speaking, you pay attention to your body only if it hurts.

B. Voluntarily notice your body at random times all day long, just for fun. (You'll never have a better friend than your physical body.)

A. Before going to sleep at night, you can't wait to pray (or worry) over your two favorite problems.

B. Before going to sleep at night, notice your body. You can simply pay attention. "Dearest body, how you doing? How do you feel?" That body has just supported a whole day's worth of activity. Would it be so terrible to send it a quick "Thank you?"

Done with All Three Choices?

Excellent. So, did you perhaps notice a pattern there?

Choice A was always the space-out choice.

Choice B was always the grounding choice.

But, ha! You figured that out early on, didn't you?

Whatever your recent choices have been — in life, not just with this quiz — you can start fresh now. Which kind of life would you prefer for yourself? (Prefer in terms of consequences.)

Why Centering Is Not Grounding

Many of my students have been told that the solution to many of life's problems is "to find your center" or "to move into your center." You too? Then admit it. Don't you have trouble remembering to do this?

Bosh! Don't blame your memory. Blame the very concept of "CENTERING."

What's wrong with that? You don't possess only one center. You have many, remember?

So what happens when a person tries to center? If you find this easy and helpful, more power to you. But usually trying to center means moving consciousness to the one category where you feel most comfortable.

Sure, this strategy is preferable to paying attention to all the other people in the room. Still, if you're out of balance within yourself, centering within that one category will only worsen the imbalance.

Centering is like saying, "I have a store where I can go to recharge and buy breath mints. It's called Emotion World."

(Substitute whichever category of yourself *used* to be your main specialty before you started using this 30-Day Plan.)

Actually, you're not just one store. You're a huge franchise. You happen to own:

1. **Mind World**
2. **Body World**
3. **Spirit World**
4. **Intellect World**
5. **Soul World**
6. **Emotion World and**
7. **Environment World**

So don't limit your sense of who-am-I to one of those stores. And definitely don't confuse any form of centering with fully grounding yourself. The latter requires visiting Body World, Mind World, Soul World and Environment World.

Most unskilled empaths, having the habit of being over-subjective, prefer Emotion World, Intellect World and/or Spirit World.

Therefore, don't just center yourself. Ground yourself. Do this even though the idea of getting up close and personal with Body World plus Environment World can bring up a raging fear of jail.

Get out of Jail Free

Ever play Monopoly? Then you know the thrill of a *Get Out of Jail Free* card. Real life involves playing a game, too (hopefully, not a bored game). Alas, many of us empaths forget that we ever agreed to play the game of living on earth. Instead we feel as though we've been thrown in jail.

Why? Life on earth is gross. Timing is slow. We must poop — and this time I'm not referring here to The Big Analogy. Some of us earthling empaths are so grossed out by life that guess what happens? We resist being in our bodies with all our might. Yet bodies aren't just something to keep around grudgingly, like a pesky kid brother.

Embrace Your Human Life. Grounding Helps

Grounding more could really change your life. Yet I just know some of you Brave Explorers aren't quite convinced yet of the need for full grounding. Here's a deeper perspective that could help.

This place I call "Earth School" is easy to love but easier to hate. The place is sooooooooo darned slow. Actually, it is slow for a reason. At our quaint little academy, various illusions and tempos enhance the learning.

- Our bodies appear to be *who* we are, although really we are energy beings having a human experience.
- Our bodies appear to be *separate* from the bodies of other people, plants, animals, etc. – ridiculous since, as you very well know, unskilled empaths fly in and out of other people's subtle bodies constantly. (For more information about how separate bodies are an illusion, ask your friendly neighborhood quantum physicist.)
- *Fear and pain* seemingly threaten to "kill" our bodies. Actually, your soul is indestructible. You will always be living in some body, somewhere. (Ask your friendly neighborhood past-life regression professional.)

Here is what I've found, helping empaths for decades. You may fear grounding most because, seemingly, it would isolate you more than ever from God.

Fighting the illusions of earth, many an empath does loads of unskilled empath merges, constantly moving in and out of other people's auras. This feels comforting, even if afterwards you bring back other people's STUFF into your aura.

But here's the bigger truth about living on earth. You're already connected to God and the rest of humanity. Full willingness to be human — without holding back — will help you to enjoy that connection more.

Already you may have noticed that living with your empath gift(s) turned OFF helps you to become more comfy in your body and environment. Gone are the days when you connected to others only as God's humble (and, possibly, frantic) servant. Then you would merge away constantly, picking up random STUFF. Now you get to calmly establish a real-life identity as a human being.

Here at Earth School, each of our words and actions will produce consequences. These show up in what happens to us, our health, relationships, the amount of roadkill encountered while driving down life's highway. In order for Earth to be effective as a school, we must be willing to accept these out-pictured consequences as if they were real, even important.

Given how life here works, choosing to be born as an empath was heroically brave. Look at the faces and bodies, even the auras, of most people who evolve at Earth School over the decades.

By age five, the glow is usually gone. By mid-life, most of us look like we've been twirled around in a food processor. By 65 and beyond, many of us develop faces that look like beat-up hiking boots.

Who are we very evolved souls who incarnate at Earth School? Yes, we're all a little bit nutty. Beyond that, we're tough. Determined to evolve further, doing our best in this highly challenging world. More power to us, even if most of us don't credit our full learning until the big life review at the end!

Unskilled empaths suffer *more* than most, even as skilled empaths suffer *less* than most. Why? Think consequences. What consequences flow when we empaths don't fully accept being here? About as bad as they *should* be!

So don't fear caring too much about your body or other aspects of human life. Will grounding cut you off from God? Will you risk losing Oneness with people, plants and animals? Brave Explorer, I'm here to tell you, this can't possibly happen.

Big perspective: Earth School's illusions won't last. At the end of this life you'll be outta here, feeling much lighter, as if all that dieting had finally worked. Even before you entered this lifetime, you were a big, evolved consciousness. Otherwise you couldn't have come in as an empath, period. Life at Earth School as an empath is designed to add to your spiritual stature, not diminish it.

Immediate perspective: It is totally safe to jump in. Starting today, you can fully inhabit your body, your surroundings, your human connections with people. Doing this, you'll evolve faster, not slower. Ironically your spiritual connection will grow far stronger.

Your Assignment for Day 25

Resolve to play here on earth as a good sport, okay?

Otherwise, what's your alternative? I would never recommend suicide… but you might wish to seek seclusion by locking yourself in Zachary 's bathroom for the next 10 years or so.

Otherwise, explore becoming a good sport. Be here now. Be here fully, which requires grounding.

Your assignment for today is to do at least three things from our Big List for Grounding. Or else find other ways to get grounded. These can be variations on what you already do. Just be sure to include at least half an hour of physical exercise daily, because your body will accept no substitute.

DAY 26

Greed

Greed and vanity no longer are fashionable sins, which is a pity. Ask Meg. Once upon a past lifetime, she worked for the Catholic church. She sold "indulgences." Depending on how well people controlled the seven deadly sins, indulgences became excellent income streams for Meg. That's one reason to like greed.

Of course, post-modern culture gives us plenty of other reasons. Advertisers are paid to persuade us that although greed is good, more greed is better.

Actually, the very moment in life when you're thinking, "I like this and want a lot more" may be the precise moment when your inner self has been trying to signal you that "I've had enough already. More would be a mistake."

Only most of us never have learned how to read those signals. Really, when was the last time that you saw a TV commercial for… nothing but satisfaction and gratitude.

Outsmart Greed

For a skilled empath, the moment when you feel "I want more" or "I want faster" is precisely the time to pause. And. Take. A. Breath.

Ask inside, "What's happening inside me right now?"

If you do this, very often you'll hear/see/feel, "I've had enough. What I have now is plenty. All I need do is stop and enjoy what I have." That's the antidote to greed, awareness of enough. Sometimes this is called "gratitude," other times "smart." But what if your best word for it is "hard"?

Getting Past Greed

Why does greed matter so much to an empath? You're close, so very close, to mastering the fine art of turning your empath gift(s) OFF as a matter of habit. Through your grounded lifestyle, your chakras are becoming more balanced. Grounding can improve relationships and your financial prospects, too. So you may have been noticing some pretty sweet results.

Soon — day after tomorrow, actually — I'll show you how to jet-propel your consciousness into another person, full force, a.k.a. turning your empath gift(s) ON.

How fascinating will that be, doing Skilled Empath Merge at will? I consider it the biggest fun you can have with your clothes on. But even then, will you feel as though you have traveled enough?

Sure, unless you give way to that last little smidge of habitual greed. It's the shadow side of enthusiasm. Teaching workshops, I've found that greed can arise in ways that don't make much sense consciously. Here are some examples:

First, Zachary. Greed shows up when, midway through the morning meeting, Zachary starts multi-tasking. He thinks he's being oh-so-cool, checking messages while he listens to class with just one ear.

What doesn't he know? Using only part of your mind, you can't succeed at empath TURN OFF techniques. Or TURN ON techniques. You know why, don't you? Which (intellect) part of his mind-body-spirit-intellect-soul-emotions-environment self... does Zachary use when multi-tasking, anyway?

Next, Jocelyn wants to be the class superstar. So she's reading ahead, skimming, impatient to bypass the boring parts and get to the good stuff.

What doesn't she know? A skill is not just an idea but something to experience. Preparation and refinement can be necessary for introducing a genuinely new experience.

That's certainly true about becoming a Skilled Empath. To complete your training fully, settle into the here and now. Follow the sequence of instruction. Every aspect of it has been designed for a reason.

Greed means wanting to have more than you have. More than the others in the class. Or faster than other people "plodding" through a 30-Day Plan. Maybe you're immune to these kinds of greed. But just in case…

Seven Lively Greed Reducers

Here are seven simple Reducers to help break old habits of greed that might impact you as an empath. If you like, think of this technique collection as an antidote to the Seven Deadly Sins.

Each Reducer can help you to feel more serene, enjoying your life as it is, which also helps you to keep your empath gift(s) OFF.

Read through as much of the list as you like. Then choose one — only one — technique to do at a time. Pushing yourself to do all seven simultaneously might be greedy. It certainly would be impossible.

1. Spend one minute thinking about things you are grateful for. (If you do this aloud, you'll intensify the gratitude.)
2. Jump-start full awareness of your *physical body* — in case it has been left behind in your quest for more-more-more. Give yourself a well-placed, gentle pinch. Once that pinch ends, let yourself notice: "Here and now, my body is a source of bliss."
3. Jump-start full awareness of your *mind* — in case it has been marginalized yet again in pursuit of "There's gotta be more."
4. Jump-start full use of your *intellect* — in case it has been bored. Plain vanilla here-and-now can be full of fascination. To stir up the fun, ask one question at a time.

5. Jump-start full awareness of your *emotions* — in case they are stuck on something un-pleasurable which causes you to want more, more, more of something different. (Might some residual greed have you demanding that every moment be the emotional equivalent of eating candy?) Gently acknowledge your current emotion, whatever it is, by asking yourself, "What do I feel right now?" Then notice it. Don't try to change it. Simple, loving acknowledgment with your conscious mind can help you plenty.
6. Jump-start your *soul* connection — in case it has been dozing. Make a wish. The nature of your soul is perfection, delight, freedom, plenty. Wishing helps your soul to speak to the rest of you.
7. And, of course, you can always use this powerful new whole-self technique: Take a deep breath. Then ask yourself, "What is fun for me right now?" Whatever you find, it's highly unlikely that it will be the greed slogan, "I need more."

Your Assignment for Day 26

As your empath coach, would it be too much if I asked you to clean up every bit of habitual greed? Hmmm, that might be asking too much. Might even be considered greedy on my part!

So let's make today's assignment simple. Just for one day, the next 24 hours, flag any habitual greed that drives you away from what you were doing. Whatever you're doing today, either do it or not — nothing in between. When you've done something long enough, move on officially, full force.

Grounding choices, as discussed yesterday, are important. But apart from making those wise choices, you can only *stay* grounded if you develop the habit of turning your empath gift(s) OFF and enjoying yourself in the moment. Without greed.

DAY 27

Room of Requirement

As of today, you officially own the necessary skills of an empath. You know what your empath gift(s) are. Plus you know how to keep them turned OFF. In this new lifestyle, everyone in the room is important, yourself included. And, with a slight shift of awareness, you can transform yourself into The Most Important Person in the Room.

Now let's see how relaxed you can be about this new way of life. Greed is going, going, gone. But do you have old habits of self-protectiveness or hiding that are no longer needed? To be perfectly safe and secure as an empath, all you really need is to be yourself, using the power of your consciousness.

Choose to be grounded. Let that consciousness fill up that full Bingo card. That, plus all the other skills you've been mastering, will help you to be yourself a way that comes across to others as natural and powerful.

But what if you're still worried? What if you want one more something to help shield yourself from taking on STUFF? As a skilled empath, some days you know you'll be dealing with difficult people, like Roscoe's girlfriend Tiger. Isn't there any extra precaution you can take? Sure! First, here's an introduction.

Hogwarts Self-Study

Thank you, J.K. Rowling for all the education I've received from Hogwarts. I know you didn't write all those Harry Potter books as do-it-yourself manuals. But thanks to you, I have learned a lot about banishing boggarts and conjuring up a patronus. Mostly I'm in love with your concept of a "Room of Requirement."

Even a squib (someone woefully untalented at magic) can conjure one up easily. All you need is a need. Once you make your request, this special room will take form exactly the way you require it to be.

Create a Room of Requirement

Ideally, you'll create this Room of Requirement *before* you have contact with a difficult person like Tiger, the mud wrestler.

Otherwise, excuse yourself for a moment and use a restroom stall as an emergency fix-up place. With practice, you can create an empath's Room of Requirement in less than one minute.

1. **Prepare to go within. Sit comfortably and close your eyes.**
2. **Notice how it feels to be you right now. Anything you notice is fine. Whatever you're noticing is about you, and that's the point.**
3. **Imagine, visualize or simply think about standing outside a Room of Requirement. This could be a complete building or a cozy apartment. It could be simple or fancy. It could be shaped like your body, a pyramid, igloo, etc. Make the walls any color and material you like. And let's emphasize that word like. Since the décor comes absolutely free of charge, indulge yourself.**
4. **Be sure to add a front door through which you can enter. Then go inside.**
5. **As you stand inside this Room of Requirement, again notice how it feels to be you.**
6. **Bring in the Divine Being of your choice. As always, no worship or special rituals are required.**

7. After offering any greeting you like, and feeling the response, ask, "Will you please help me today?"
8. You're sure to receive an okay. Divine Beings give unconditional love and support whenever we ask. But don't wait to receive some loud, official "***Y***E***S***." Awaiting something like a cartoon sledgehammer that knocks Tweety Bird to the ground! Any technique or prayer that you do involving a Divine Being needs no big drama in order to count as real.
9. Continuing, say, "Please help me to feel better about myself, my human self."
10. Soon something will happen. Count aloud from one to three. Then your Room of Requirement will quickly shrink in size, shrinking more with each number, until it merges with your skin. Okay, say those numbers now: 1, 2, 3.
11. Now you're surrounded by this miniaturized Room of Requirement. How far does it stick out? No thicker than a dewdrop. And that's all you need do in order to receive this form of protection. Open your eyes.

Most days, you won't feel the need to create a Room of Requirement. But it's nice to have the skill when you want it, fine use for some of your 20 Daily Minutes of Technique Time, Tops.

Congratulations on learning how to create and use your own Room of Requirement. Now you have that extra bit of personal protection, as needed.

Your Assignment for Day 27

Adding our Room of Requirement technique is an optional change to your routine. Just for today, play with it once.

The biggest protection, however, is simpler — even — than creating a Room of Requirement.

As an empath, your biggest protection is just being yourself, empath gift(s) turned OFF — you in all your human glory.

Mobilize that strong self of yourself by having fun, human fun!

DAY 28

Magic Picture

Your first official Skilled Empath Merge — yes, you'll do it today.

You're ready now. Not only will you stay in better balance than if you'd tried today's technique earlier. The quality of your experience will be better. And the information you receive will be more accurate.

It's like the reason why psychiatrists must go through therapy before becoming qualified to practice. *Helping other people, you can only go as deep as you have gone into yourself.*

Deep/shallow: You've been playing around with these concepts while exploring what it means to become The Most Important Person in The Room. You have learned to relish, in depth, each category of your mind-body-spirit-intellect-soul-emotions-environment.

Today's turn ON technique for your empath gift(s) can take you *that* deeply and widely into the person with whom you do the empath merge.

So roll up your sleeves. Loosen your belt. Make whatever adjustments to clothing signify your readiness to start something special. Zachary, for instance, needs to snap his suspenders so they make a rich twanging sound.

Learning your first technique for Skilled Empath Merge, you will need a full 30 minutes — uninterrupted. Unless you have that time right now, stop reading. Return when you do have that time. Most of it will be needed for preparation. Doing the technique itself will take you 10 minutes or less.

So Prepare for Magic

The official name of this technique is "Magic Picture."

Nothing about today's technique is difficult. You'll succeed, so long as you go with me step by step. Like it or not, there is no way to do Safe, Deep and Skilled Empath Merge for Dummies.

Your Magical Supplies

For starters, Magic Picture will require certain supplies:

1. The previously-mentioned 30 minutes of your precious time
2. A room where you will be uninterrupted by cell phone, pets, a panting roommate who just can't wait to have sex with you, etc.
3. A recording device, whether that be an electronic machine to record your voice or good old-fashioned pen and paper
4. A certain kind of photograph...

You'll find that photos are great for doing Skilled Empath Merge. Since photos don't talk back or giggle; they won't rush you or make you self-conscious in any way.

This holds true whether you choose a photo of somebody you know well or a total stranger.

Find a Suitable Photo for Skilled Empath Merge

What makes the best kind of photo for doing the Magic Picture technique.

- Choose a photo that shows only one person.
- That would be a human person, not a poodle or extra-terrestrial, not a cartoon of Daffy Duck.

- And, please, no cute cropping that chops off the person's forehead.
- Your person must be facing the camera at a nice clear front angle. This image should go all the way down to the waist. Longer is fine, shorter is not.
- Nothing about the person's physical appearance should be distracting. So probably the person in your photo will be wearing clothing. Now, Zachary has a real fondness for the swimsuit issue of Sports Illustrated; apparently he is soooo into those cute bathing suits. But enjoying photos like these would be considered a different technique.
- For pity's sake, choose a photo of somebody nice, not necessarily perfect but, please, not revolting. For instance, avoid empath-merging with that politician you love to hate from the front page of today's newspaper.
- Not to be too demanding, your photo should also be larger than a postage stamp.
- You'll be learning about the person *at the time of the photograph.* If you want to do Skilled Empath Merge to learn about Troy as an adult, don't use his baby picture, no matter how adorable Find something current.

Whew, now we have all that settled. Next up, let's practice the correct physical positioning for this technique.

Next, What about You?

Treat the process of Skilled Empath Merge with respect and you'll receive the most accurate information possible. Another way to put it: You can be of service to the greatest extent possible.

Also, doing Skilled Empath Merge properly will protect you against Imported STUFF.

I've developed many different techniques for becoming a Master Empath. This one is perfect for a beginner. Start by paying attention to your physical position.

Do what you can to ensure you will not be interrupted by a phone, a person, or anything else. Take away cigarettes or gum. Keep your attention undivided.

Now, sit comfortably in a chair, feet on the floor, legs not crossed, arms not crossed.

Hold your photo in one hand and lift it up until you can see the person in your picture at eye level.

Is your photo on a computer screen? Any laptop belongs off your lap. Adjust positions relative to where you sit to get the screen image at eye level. Do whatever scrolling, etc., is needed so that you can sit across from that image comfortably, head erect and eyes looking straight ahead.

Most of us are used to looking down at pictures. That won't work well for any empath merge technique. (Your brain processes information differently when you look on the level versus when you look down.)

Can you look over now, at eye level, and see your person's forehead? How about the neck? Even a short neck will do.

Excellent! Photo practice is over, so put your photo down, or turn away from your screen, and keep reading.

Prepare to Record Your Skilled Empath Merge

Already you know that you will be recording your experiences with Magic Picture. Probably you'll just scribble quick notes on a sheet of paper, although you could make a sound recording.

To give yourself the best experience possible, tell yourself right now that this recording process will be quick and easy. Ideally, making notes during a technique like this is just like drooling. No need to pretty anything up, more like a spontaneous, automatic outpouring of words.

Decide right now that when you do scribble-writing you will:

- ◦ Never stop to check that your writing is pretty.
- ◦ Forget about making grammatically correct sentences.
- ◦ Make just enough of a scribble to be readable later. Scribble-writing!

As part of your preparation, please position your pen and paper, or electronic device, so that you're ready to record.

Sometimes an empath will feel a bit shy about doing a new technique and position consciousness unhelpfully at a critical time: by slowly opening up a notebook, searching for the right page, taking out the prettiest purple pen, using excellent calligraphy skills, etc.

Don't do that to yourself. Be prepared, then trust yourself enough to be sloppy, okay?

You're Preparing for a Historic Moment, Actually

Historic because this will be your first depth experience of Skilled Empath Merge. So let's pause briefly to consider this historic moment in your life.

Do you remember our definition of what it means to be an empath? An empath has at least one significant, trainable gift for directly experiencing what it is like to be another person.

Now you are finally about to use that ability. On purpose. And in a way where you are protected from picking up STUFF. Before our 30-Day Plan, you did plenty of unskilled empath merges, not nearly the same thing as using your talent on purpose.

Instead you did little bits, not-quite-consciously, here and there. Playing with your Space Dial has shown you how to consciously use your gift(s) better, but even a 10 on that dial delivers about 5% of the oomph of a dedicated Skilled Empath Merge.

Yes, you read that right. What you're about to do is a uniquely powerful use of your empath gift(s).

Through, Not With

Here's a secret about *all* techniques for Skilled Empath Merge, not just the one you're learning today. After you prepare properly, you will purposely switch ON the experience through one of your human senses.

"Through" is different from "with."

You see, your experience will not depend on a sensation you would have directly *with* your hand or eye or ear. Instead, consciousness flows *through* one or more of your senses.

So don't expect a physical experience. Instead, accept an experience of consciousness consisting of bits and bytes of information. This info flows through, or by means of, your physical self. Because you're human, one of your physical senses will always be involved in a technique for Skilled Empath Merge.

You're sure to have favorites among those senses, so that once you learn a range of techniques, you'll be able to identify whichever techniques for Skilled Empath Merge that you like best. Ultimately, all you need is one. Other techniques can be used occasionally just to bring variety.

Magic Picture is a touchy-feely technique. Tomorrow you'll learn one that combines seeing with touch and has a huge array of variations. In my more advanced book, *The Master Empath*, you can find extra techniques for Skilled Empath Merge that involve much, much more variety, plus many practical applications.

But for now, we've got to start somewhere. So let's roll up our sleeves and prepare for flow through!

The Yin and Yang of Your Hands

Doing Magic Picture, you will use one hand as a research tool. But which one?

Interlace your fingers. One of those thumbs will be on top.

Raise the hand attached to that thumb. This is your dominant hand. If you like, from now on you can call this hand "Mr. Yang." He's great for sending out healing energy.

Doing an Empath Merge isn't about sending healing energy, however. For this exercise, Mr. Yang will show his prowess simply by holding up your photo.

So raise your other hand. Meet "Ms. Yin," the hand with more feminine energy.

Keep track of which hand is which. It matters for all techniques of Skilled Empath Merge that involve touch.

A Special Exception

Okay, what if you're a rebel, like Meg? So you could naturally put either thumb on top. Or else you fudge things just a little, being rightfully proud of your dexterity. Congratulations. Now we know you're special.

So let's move on. Check out which pinky finger is on the bottom. That pinky belongs to Ms. Yin. Got it? Good.

Next, "Wad Position"

Doing the Magic Picture technique, you'll hold Ms. Yin in a particular position which I call "Wad." Let's practice.

1. Extend your thumb and all your fingers out straight. (You could consider this the opposite of making a fist.)
2. Cupping your hand slightly, all five digits will be together.
3. Hold that hand up and look between the fingers. If you're doing Wad properly, you won't see space but, instead, a nice soft line where one finger makes contact with another. Even your thumb tip does something similar, lying against the base of your index finger.

About this cupped hand, is it held rigidly, causing pain? No, that would be a different technique. Personally, I'm not into that technique. Our technique is for making an *easy, comfortable, useful* Wad.

INTRODUCING Research Positions

Magic Picture enables you to research a person from the inside out. Four locations are especially interesting for doing this research, so I call them "Research Positions."

Each position is centered at a particular body part:
- The forehead
- The throat
- The chest
- The ribcage

See our illustration on the opposite page. Ours features beautiful Lexi.

Don't feel shy about staring at Lexi or anyone else. Don't think you must be super-precise, either. You're aiming your hand for an empath merge, not doing brain surgery.

These four Research Positions will aim your consciousness at certain chakras, entry points into a person's aura. When that chosen direction is combined with the rest of a particular technique, your consciousness will have liftoff.

PRACTICING Research Positions

Before we actually do this Magic Picture, let's do one final practice. Rehearse the following physical positions, please.

And when you do this, please don't be concerned with energy flows or subjective anything.

We're just getting you familiar with where to place Ms. Yin, using Wad Position.

Research Positions

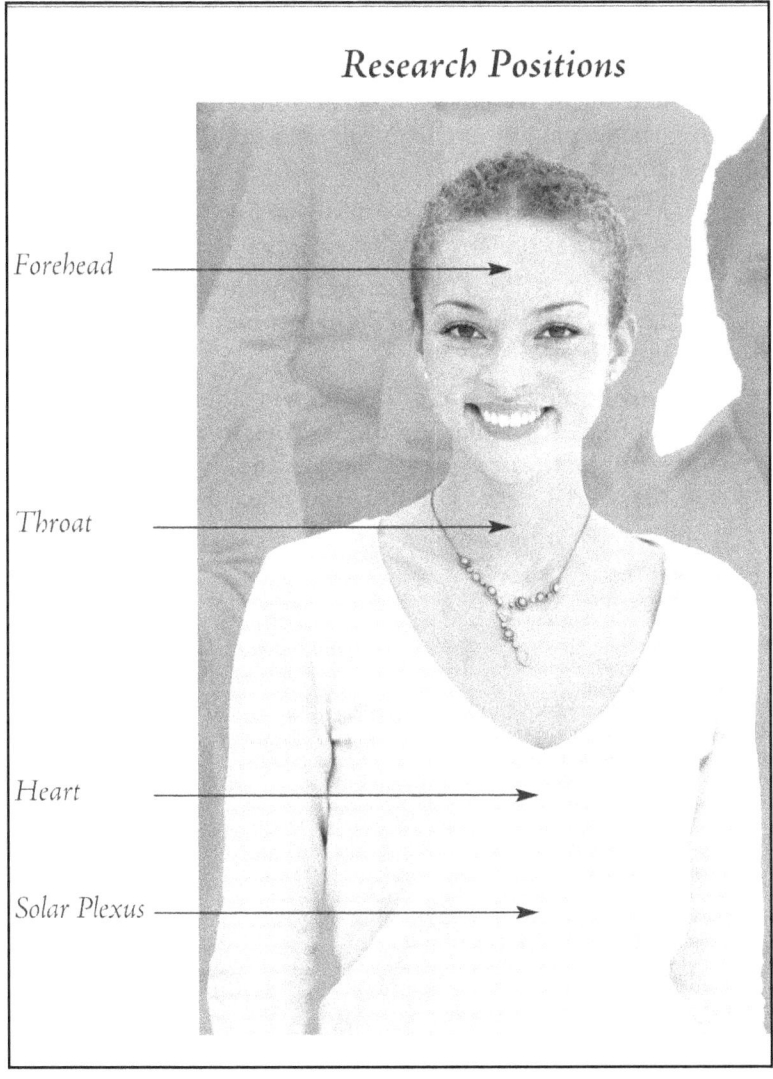

Using Mr. Yang, hold the photo you're using for Magic Picture up to eye level.

Now you're reading to practice your Research Positions.

1. Hold Ms. Yin sideways, in Wad Position, a couple of inches away from the photo (or the screen containing the photo).
2. Aim your palm at the person's forehead. Pointing your fingers toward the right or left? You choose. Experiment and decide whichever angle is more comfortable. This is what, from now on, we'll call "Research Position at the Forehead."
3. Move Ms. Yin down a bit until you find "Research Position at the Throat Chakra."
4. Next, move down to "Research Position at Heart Chakra Level." That would be in the center of the body, at the breastbone.
5. Finally, move down to "Research Position at the Ribcage." The Solar Plexus Chakra is located in the center of the body, about halfway between the waist and the heart-level position you just practiced.

Is all your preparation complete. Yes!

Magic Picture

Finally you're ready to use this technique for Skilled Empath Merge. Please read through the following instructions. Then go back and start at the beginning, proceeding step by step. (Open your eyes and peeking at the words as needed.)

1. Bring out the most important ingredient for this recipe: You. Sit comfortably, back erect, head not supported. Close your eyes and notice what it feels like to be you. That could be anything about your mind-body-spirit-intellect-soul-emotions-environment.
2. Paying attention to yourself is effortless but real. To make sure you've really made contact, shift your consciousness to a *second* category of your mind-body-spirit-intellect-soul-emotions-environment.
3. Get Big. Think the name "God," or another name you'd prefer, so long as it's your highest source of inspiration. (One quick thought does it. You're connected.)
4. Take a deep breath, settling into this subtly expanded version of being yourself.
5. Set an intention, such as "I'm ready to gain more wisdom." Think the thought once and consider the job done. You have directed your consciousness perfectly.
6. Hold up your Magic Picture with Mr. Yang. Move Ms. Yin into Research Position at the Forehead. Think this question: "What can I learn from this person about connecting to God?"
7. Immediately close your eyes and take a slow, deep breath. Take another. Then return to normal breathing.
8. Whatever you are experiencing now, in any way, is about your research subject. Open your eyes just enough to record your impressions on your notebook (or whatever). Remember, whatever you experience now *counts,* so make a quick note.

9. Move to Research Position at the Throat. Think this question: "Which strengths does this person bring to communicating in close relationships?" Repeat Steps 7-8.
10. Half-time break! Put your picture down. Stretch. Repeat Steps 1-5.
11. Move to Research Position at the Heart. Think this question: "Which strengths does this person bring to emotional connection to others?" Repeat Steps 7-8.
12. Move to Research Position at the Solar Plexus. Ask, "What is a gift of this person's soul for using power?" Repeat Steps 7-8.
13. Inwardly, say something like, "Thank you. Now this technique is over."
14. Return to the experience of being you. Notice at least two things about your mind-body-spirit-intellect-soul-emotions-environment.
15. Open your eyes. Consider your empath gift(s) officially turned OFF and rejoin your environment as The Most Important Person in The Room.

Done! Applause!

Hmmm, what's the sound of one hand clapping? Maybe that depends on whether it's Mr. Yang or Ms. Yin? Figuring that out is a different technique.

Aw, I'm just getting silly now. Because I'm thrilled that you've completed your first Skilled Empath Merge.

You can do the technique again whenever you like. Just use a different photo each time. Another important point: Either you're doing Magic Picture or you're not. (And, right now, please, not! Give yourself a rest; also a little time to feel very proud of yourself.)

Get in the habit of making a clear distinction of "In Technique Time" versus "Normally being a human being, interested in life around me."

Over the past month, you've worked very hard to learn how to turn your gift(s) OFF. Now you're going back to OFF.

Feel the difference? Keep that distinction clear at every level of your being. *Either you're doing a technique to turn your gift(s) ON or else you're turning all those gift(s) OFF.*

The Magic Picture technique is like any dedicated technique for Skilled Empath Merge: Spiritually powerful. The impact on you is far more powerful than it might seem initially. Same could be said for the quality of information received while your empath circuits are ON.

Sweet Success

Bold Explorer, let's reflect on what you just accomplished. Otherwise you might miss it — which would not be because nothing happened but because what happened was so subtle. Skilled Empath Merges are done with consciousness. Movies spoil us, with their big budgets and flashy special effects. By contrast, Skilled Empath Merges are screened within you. That means all natural, deep as can be, and not flashy.

Pick up the notes you made from that Skilled Empath Merge. Look them over appreciatively. Please, start from this assumption: *I am magnificently talented at doing Skilled Empath Merge. And I just did something awesome.*

Therefore:

- No need to act like a harsh critic.
- Forget about doubting your experiences. The way this technique was set up, everything counted.
- Never repeat research that you have already done. Throat Chakra research on Mr. Turnip Face can be considered complete! Hey, only a zillion other photos in the world remain for you to research.

Did you know? The best way to have more vivid experiences in the future is to be grateful for what you just received now. In more innocent days, when you first learned to read with word literacy, you did this gratitude thing pretty darned well, remember? Now you can do this as an adult, an adult who's a skilled empath.

Guess What — Everything Counts

Once I gave a workshop for empaths where students were paired up to do Skilled Empath Merges. After doing the technique, Barbie was upset. She pulled me over to complain:

"It was just awful. Not only did nothing happen when I did your technique, but I felt fat and blobby, like I weighed a hundred extra pounds.

"All of a sudden, for no reason at all, just being in the workshop made me nervous, as if I had social anxiety or something weird like that.

"And I don't mean to brag, but usually people call me intelligent. Doing your technique, my mind became dull. Really, I don't think I have ever felt so fat. And blobby. And stupid."

Oh, the tact needed! Have you guessed? Barbie was giving a great description about how it felt, temporarily experiencing what it was like to be her partner.

So I'm not kidding. Once you get to Step 8 of Magic Picture, everything counts. Usually your experiences will be positive and fascinating, but not always. Don't let the success of your Skilled Empath Merge... sneak up on you.

Your Assignment for Day 28

Your assignment for today is to do Magic Picture once more, only researching a *different* person. Use the *same* four Research Positions.

DAY 29

The Master Technique

Fat and blobby, tall and perky, or giggly and silly and wise — how did you wind up feeling when you did your homework yesterday? Doing your first full-blown technique for Skilled Empath Merge, you began to jet-propel yourself into the experience of Otherness.

Never will you be able to anticipate how another person's Otherness will be. The experience is always unique. It differs completely from using emotional intelligence, expression reading, or other superficial approaches. Remember Day 23, when we discussed deep vs. shallow?

Exploring someone's façade is another popular ways to learn what someone is really like; for an empath it's right at the shallow end of the swimming pool. A FAÇADE is a personality projection, how a person tries to appear in public. In every social relationship, each party wears a façade.

Hairstyle, makeup, etc. can add impact to a façade. Personally, I think it's sad when people get better clothes or a "makeover" and then proclaim, "I'm a new person." Sure, it's true... if that person is so shallow that inner experience goes no deeper than façade. Today's vanity culture is all about conflating the surface of life into "all that is." But you are daring to be counter-culture, seeking truth all the way to its innermost parts.

Otherness means the direct experience of what makes a person distinctive. During Skilled Empath Merge, consciousness moves way beyond surface projections like façade. You wake up to find yourself inside the person's reality, experiencing Otherness.

Want a hilarious new hobby? Try doing Magic Picture with a photo where the model is supposedly meditating, sleeping, kissing, or enjoying the taste of food. The model's inner experience while posing is sure to be different. Attention is more likely devoted to personal matters, like "Does my chest look good?"

Bam! Courtesy of a Skilled Empath Merge, you have tweaked an illusion. It's like Zachary snapping his suspenders. Notice the rich twanging sound.

Transcending the efforts people make to "think outside the box," you can *travel* there in consciousness.

Usually, people live inside their own boxes. Doing Skilled Empath Merge briefly brings your awareness outside yourself, into the Otherness of another person's box. Such a privilege!

So much for inspiration. How about experience? Let's say that you do a Skilled Empath Merge with Zachary. You might notice characteristics like these:

- Physically, his face feels tight around the mouth, and he has this cute default expression of sneering.
- Emotionally, he appears cut off from people. Actually, Zachary goes through more emotions than an outsider might guess. And he does have Emotional Oneness.
- Intellectually, Zachary is quite exhausted right now. Who wouldn't be, favoring his emotions constantly, then using his intellect to try to calm all those feelings down?
- What's Zachary's biggest secret? He loves insects. Gotta love a man who has spent much of his life doing spontaneous, unskilled empath merges with ants. Talented as an Animal Empath, he happens to specialize in insects. Golly, before starting our 30-Day Plan, perhaps you thought you had been doing a thankless form of volunteer work!

About that Volunteer Work

Whenever you do an empath merge, skilled or not, it's volunteer work. Before I teach you the Master Technique for doing Skilled Empath Merge at will, let's consider that. Fun aside, what's the point of doing volunteer work as a skilled empath?

As a skilled empath, you can turn your gift(s) ON for service. Say that you work in a helping profession, like being an acupuncturist or massage therapist.

You might do one Skilled Empath Merge with your "client" right at the start of your session. After that, go back to being yourself. Use your regular professional skill set for helping that person.

How many skill sets you have accumulated throughout your life! And now, of course, your list includes keeping your empath gift(s) nicely turned OFF most of the time, Space Dial set at 1, using the "Take It" technique, etc.

Service done in this way will be far more effective than service done in personal burnout mode, Space Dial at 10, heaping STUFF from others into your already STUFF-packed aura.

Living as a skilled empath, you'll find many practical uses... high-functioning uses... for the amazingly deep gift(s) you have had your whole life. This is especially true when you add the ability to do Skilled Empath Merges.

Many more people know about autism than about being wired as an empath. Experts may call a particular autistic child "high-functioning" because that child is able to adapt well to life among those who aren't autistic.

Empaths, too, can be high-functioning. Only the concept of high- or low-functioning relates to exceptional abilities rather than a disability. Unskilled empaths are low-functioning, since each empath gift become a basis for suffering. Unskilled empaths appear to function normally as human beings but they're not using their capacity to safely and clearly experience Otherness.

During our 30-Day Plan, you have learned to become The Most Important Person in the Room, turning your empath gift(s) OFF. This makes you a moderately-functioning empath. Only when you gain skill at turning your empath gift(s) ON, as part of a balanced life, do you become a truly high-functioning empath. Then your contribution to life can become extraordinary.

Be a High-Functioning Empath

Society today has brings us few role models for what it means to be a high-functioning empath, what we have been calling all along a fully "skilled empath," meaning somebody with the default of empath gift(s) OFF, and who also can do Skilled Empath Merge at will.

You are becoming that new kind of person, which prepares you for remarkable service to humanity.

SERVICE to others as a high-functioning empath is like having someone you really respect (Archangel Raphael? Your favorite politician? Maybe a movie star? God?) whisper the most important secrets about your the person you're learning about. Then you proceed to do service based on that deepest possible knowledge.

As a high-functioning empath, turning your gift(s) ON with skill will greatly deepen your **WISDOM**. At will, you can plunge into the direct experience of Otherness, a completely different way to be. Think, feel, and learn inside the box — somebody else's box.

Remember the example of doing an Empath Merge with a model in some silly ad? That can **SMASH SPIRITUAL ILLUSIONS** for you in a way that is not inferior to Buddha's process beneath his famed banyan tree.

Or you could do a Skilled Empath Merge with a photo of your biggest hero. Get yourself amazing **INSPIRATION**!

Do you have someone in your life whom you have tried to **FORGIVE** but just can't? A Skilled Empath Merge might help.

Opening up **YOUR HEART OF COMPASSION** — that's my fancy name for the soul-level wisdom you can gain every time that you choose to do a Skilled Empath Merge.

How about doing the Magic Picture technique on a photo of yourself 10 years ago? It's no science-fiction time travel. Instead, use this real and very practical way to **UNDERSTAND YOURSELF** with uncanny accuracy. And the better you know yourself, as a high-functioning empath, the greater your reach when giving service to others.

Preparing to graduate from our 30-Day Plan, today you'll expand your service by learning my Master Technique for Empath Merge. As with learning Magic Picture, we'll start by practicing different aspects of physical position.

Your Latest Research Tool

Eyes are about to become your latest tool for Skilled Empath Merge For our Master Technique, you will look at one particular body part at a time, the visual equivalent of what you did yesterday when putting your hand into Research Position. Using eyes, you will have one major DO and several important DON'Ts.

DO aim your eyes at one body part at a time. *On the following page*, there's an illustration of Cute Guy researching Gail's forehead, so we'll use her as an example.

During Empath Merge, DON'T use your eyes for any of these other purposes:

- Deciding if you like Gail's clothes, jewelry, and makeup.
- Evaluating if Gail is good or nice or not.
- Reading Gail's mood from facial expression and body language.

The following little technique can prepare you do your best at Skilled Empath Merge.

Aim Your Eyes for Research

Refresh Your Inner Screen

Use this simple technique to gain clarity, like when you're reading online and seek freshly updated information. Only this is a quick way to wake up your own consciousness.

1. Close your eyes.
2. Take a deep breath.
3. Think this intention once: "I'm ready to receive more wisdom."
4. Take another deep breath and know that you have been given a fresh new start.
5. Open your eyes.

Refresh Your Inner Screen is so easy. Do it whenever you want a fresh start for a technique of Skilled Empath Merge.

You'll Need a Live Person for the Master Technique

Yes, this super-flexible Master Technique must be done with a real, live person in the room with you. Let's call this person "Lexi." (See her illustration in our last chapter for a reminder of Research Positions.)

And now comes the rest of your preparation.

For the Master Technique, you'll two additional Research Positions to your repertoire, belly and leg. For "belly," choose any spot on the abdominal area. For "leg," choose either leg and then pick one spot on that leg. To brush up on which hand is "Ms. Yin," and refresh your understanding of Wad Position, see our last chapter.

Use common sense, of course, in choosing your Discovery Person. Avoid doing Skilled Empath Merge with any person who strikes you as crazy, angry, high on drugs, etc. Otherwise you might have to take a lot of showers afterwards! Also, do Skilled Empath Merge on just one person at a time. (If you're not clear why, please go back and re-do Day 26.)

The Master Technique for Skilled Empath Merge

Once you've prepared, simply go step by step.

1. Close your eyes and notice at least two different things about yourself right now. Choose from categories of your mind-body-spirit-intellect-soul-emotions-environment.
2. Get Big. Think the name "God," or another name that you'd prefer as your highest source of inspiration. (One quick thought does it. You're connected.)
3. Set an intention, e.g., Think, "I choose to gain greater wisdom."
4. Jump-start a Skilled Empath Merge through one of these methods, always using Ms. Yin in Wad Position.

- Look at Lexi. Think, "When I touch my heart, this will jet-propel me inside Lexi's heart." Then place Ms. Yin palm down in the center of your chest and take a deep breath.
- Look at Lexi. Think, "When I touch my ribcage, this will jet-propel me inside Lexi's mind and intellect." Then place Ms. Yin palm down in the center of your front ribcage and take a deep breath.
- Look at Lexi. Think, "When I touch my belly, this will jet-propel me inside Lexi's gut." Then place Ms. Yin palm down in the center of your belly and take a deep breath.
- Look at Lexi. Think, "When I touch my leg, this will jet-propel me inside Lexi's body." Then place Ms. Yin palm down on one of your thighs and take a deep breath.

5. Everything that happens next counts as information about Lexi. Close your eyes to intensify your experience. Breathe deeply to turn up the volume of your inner knowing.

6. Staying connected, ask one question at a time about what is going on with Lexi. Be sure to include a positive question like, "What can I learn about [Name one aspect of life, such as "Spiritual Connection" or "Physical Coordination"] from Lexi?"
7. After asking each question, just be. Stay connected. Breathe. Count everything that happens to you now as valid information. Yes, that means any experience you are having about your mind-body-spirit-intellect-soul-emotions-environment.
8. Move your hand. Release the connection.
9. Make quick notes about what you have learned. Ideally, write do scribble-writing or make a sound recording.
10. Close your eyes. Say, "God, please remove all astral ties between myself and Lexi. Fill us up with new calmness."
11. Also say, "Thank you, God. Now this technique is over." Open your eyes. Consider your empath gift(s) officially turned OFF, and rejoin your environment as The Most Important Person in The Room.

The more you practice Skilled Empath Merge, the better you'll get at it, until the flow of experience and words is dependable. Also expect to gain trust. Although practice will help you, remember to practice in moderation: 20 Daily Minutes of Technique Time, Tops. During our 30-Day Plan you've worked hard to get your life in balance. Keep that balance, Brave Explorer.

That's your priority, no matter how much you love doing Skilled Empath Merges. Most of your waking hours, keep those empath gifts turned OFF. Comfortably OFF.

To put it another way, most of your waking hours allow yourself to be The Most Important Person in The Room. And let's be clear. Your reason to feel important is not because you have the power to move in and out of other people's consciousness but because mostly you get to be you.

A person could get carried away with this new toy. Skilled Empath Merges bring powerful shifts of experience, exploration of Otherness that would make any true science fiction buff want to drool with envy. You may be tempted to overdo.

But don't. Commit to staying balanced as a person. For the best possible quality of life, keep using all the skills developed during our previous days, and add just a wee bit of Empath Merge.

Most days, just a short time is plenty. One 30-minute practice period per day, max, for the rest of our 30-Days — and for the next 30, too. That's ideal for adding Skilled Empath Merge to your lifestyle.

In everyday situations, notice when you are becoming involved in someone else's story or energies. Are you going to make this part of your 20 Daily Minutes of Technique Time, Tops? Does another person's pressure create your emergency? Skilled Empath Merges aren't terribly different from conjugal visits, minus the commute time., etc. Choose your partner wisely.

Once you agree to this little bit of restraining order, you can safely make The Master Technique a part of your daily life.

Your Assignment for Day 29

No homework today! But you might want to play once more with The Master Technique, just for the fun of it.

Or do Magic Picture again, for exercising different empath's muscles, and then return to today's technique another day. All this would be for 20 minutes of Technique Time maximum, remember?

Otherwise, you've got plans, great plans, for your waking hours. Enjoy your magnificent human life, as The Most Important Person in The Room.

DAY 30

Completion

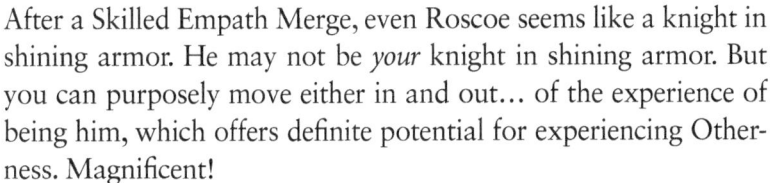

After a Skilled Empath Merge, even Roscoe seems like a knight in shining armor. He may not be *your* knight in shining armor. But you can purposely move either in and out… of the experience of being him, which offers definite potential for experiencing Otherness. Magnificent!

Brave Explorer, you have learned techniques for sampling magnificent Otherness, either in person or via photo. However well you have done so far, your clarity will only improve over time.

Gaining access to a desired experience whenever you like — that's one reason to use techniques. You don't have to wait until you haphazardly slip-and-slide into an experience of Otherness. Moreover you can do a strong Skilled Empath Merge *safely* now, without picking up any Imported STUFF. Of course, you're doing Skilled Empath Merge for reasonable amounts of time and always for a purpose, correct? And otherwise you're concentrating on being yourself, right?

I sure hope so, because that combo is the essence of being a Skilled Empath, high-functioning, having the most wonderful life. Today you complete our 30-Day Plan. Let's summarize what you have learned.

10 Ways to Live as a Skilled Empath

1. **Mostly you keep your empath gift(s) turned OFF.**

2. You do this in a natural way that wakes you up from inside, without a speck of phony or manipulative *anything*.
3. To help other people in social situations, you use a variety of normal, human skill sets — just as non-empaths do. These skills could include assertiveness, striving to balance give-and-take in relationships, and taking effective action in the outer world.
4. Gone is the old habit of assuming that helping people automatically means that you connect with them energetically and take on their STUFF.
5. Also gone is the old habit of defaulting to an over-subjective way of positioning consciousness. When something in objective life becomes a problem, you take action in the objective realm.
6. You understand that Empath Empowerment involves *subtle* shifts in how you use consciousness. Easy does it, no big effort required.
7. But should effort be required to help someone else, that's when to use the "Take It" technique, so you never have to play God while in a human body.
8. Now, when you turn your empath gift(s) ON, you're making it a quality experience.
9. By playing with the combination of OFF and ON in your day, and not doing more than 20 Minutes of Technique Time daily, you have developed balance in your life.
10. Ta da! Wherever you go, you are automatically The Most Important Person in The Room.

Enjoy your new status. Do you find it tasty? Terrific? Positively twinkling?

Graduation Quiz

Oh, I have so many questions for you, Brave Explorer. Let's turn them into an official quiz. When you answer the following questions, feel free to brag. Brag out loud or write things down. Or comment at my blog, "Deeper Perception Made Practical."

1. Thanks to Empath Empowerment, you've got more of a life now. Has anyone else noticed a change in you? Have you?
2. As of today, which are your favorite categories of mind-body-spirit-intellect-soul-emotions-environment?
3. Does any of those MBS. I see! categories still need a little more quality attention, such as dedicated time each day or, even, healing? (No shame in that, remember.)
4. Yesterday, how many times did you use The Wakeup Call? Or are you finding that you don't need to do it that often, not any more.
5. When was the last time you did Advanced Bingo, and what happened?
6. As a skilled empath, are you looking at people differently now? I mean that literally, as in our Eye Muscles technique.
7. Are you satisfied with the décor in your Room of Requirement? (You can always change it, you know.)
8. Think of a tricky ongoing relationship, one that used to be draining. How are you using your Space Dial now with this person? As a consequence, what has shifted?
9. Guilt: Comparing now to 30 days ago, do you have more guilt or less?
10. "What I do isn't enough." Comparing now to 30 days ago, do you have more of that old worry or less?
11. Your nose. Compared to 30 days ago, do you have more nose or less? (Okay, I'm kidding about that part. But this Question is a great place to talk or write about anything else you consider important about your growth as an empath.)
12. What is still a growth area — or relationship — for you?

Bold Explorer, you have a lot to be proud of, don't you! Please expect that results in your personal growth will gently trickle in. And you want it that way, rather than dramatic, eye-popping change with all the subtlety of Niagara Falls. Trust me on this one.

Magnificence

Every human being alive is, in some way, magnificent. If you weren't an empath, you might have to settle for theory about this.

I host a blog called "Deeper Perception Made Practical." Back in the day, the following comment came in from Kudzu, a poetic young man:

> *more and more i try to see others as sources of spiritual light in the firmament.*
>
> *i try to see people as soft blue glows all around me*
>
> *gratitude and humility*

Kudzu has neatly summarized three different techniques. Besides what he wrote, there are innumerable techniques for imagining a better experience of reality. And so many of us, unskilled empaths and skilled empaths alike, may sometimes find ourselves striving for a more spiritual connection to others. When I first read Kudzu's words, I could feel his tremendous yearning for more in life.

Sweet! But let's bring some discernment to balance the admiration. From your perspective as a skilled empath, what is limiting about Kudzu's techniques?

You may find it useful to distinguish techniques made from *within* your own box (like Kudzu's) to techniques about moving into another person's box entirely. Skilled Empath Merges are the ultimate way to move into another person's box. But what if, like Kudzu, one is not an empath?

Day 30. Completion

I teach techniques of Deeper Perception that anyone can do successfully. So consider these next resources:

In a previous chapter you have already played with my highly counter-culture approach to BODY LANGUAGE. Depending on whether you are an empath or not, body language can shallow you up or take you a bit deeper.

As a skilled empath, you'll find that FACE READING SECRETS® is a skill set that can be used (in person or through photos) to go outside your box and see each person's face as meaningful, highly informative, even sacred.

AURA READING THROUGH ALL YOUR SENSES® is another outside-the-box skill set. It can be used in person or through photos, revealing subtle truths that cannot be faked.

What happens when a skilled empath like you uses any form of Deeper Perception to understand the dynamics of another person's box? Except for face reading and body language, watch out! Probably you're going to switch ON your gift(s) as an empath.

That's right. Even if empath merge isn't part of the official job description, you'll probably do it. The same goes for skills like Emotional Freedom Technique (E.F.T.), Reiki healing, Energy Medicine, hypnosis, massage, teaching, nursing, being a really good receptionist — any time when you define your activity as going deeeeeeeply into experience.

Automatically, you'll start doing unskilled empathic merges. Even if it wasn't officially taught to you when you learned these skill sets. This point was touched on before in the context of studying aura reading. But let's expand this point here, since today is Completion Day.

Unless you maintain the habit of keeping your empath gifts OFF, you'll do unskilled empath merges while you give, *or receive,* any intuitive skill, service occupation, or healing modality. Please be cognizant of that possibility. Just because you can now do Skilled

Empath Merge doesn't mean that you'll never do the unskilled kind again.

So remember to use the Turn-OFF techniques you have learned throughout our 30-Day Plan.

Use them especially in conjunction with any skill set that might otherwise trigger an unskilled empath merge. In addition, as a smart precaution, here comes the final technique in our 30-Day Plan.

Helping WITHOUT Doing Unskilled Empath Merge

Before you start to comfort that family member or friend:
1. Use the skill set that does not require that you be an empath, e.g., Baking, sewing, plumbing, how to make a good sandwich.
2. Stop trying to fix human problems by using energy. Make the human-type choice.
3. Consider your empath gift(s) officially turned OFF and rejoin your environment as The Most Important Person in The Room.

Pretty simple, right?

It may also help you to remember that experiences of Skilled Empath Merge are subtle. After you have done several, you'll begin to notice contrast.

With time and more experience, your sense of contrast will become increasingly clear. Sometimes, during your Technique Time, you'll do a Skilled Empath Merge, exploring other people temporarily, using consciousness to become aware of true Otherness.

But otherwise? You'll spend your waking hours being yourself. Knowing yourself. Evolving spiritually as yourself.

Empaths, a Peek at Your Future

Being a skilled empath means so much more than Becoming The Most Important Person in the Room. You are fortified against unwitting unskilled empath merges. Altogether, you can confidently expect to play an exciting new role in life, showing the world how to live with Empath Empowerment.

Among the millions of unskilled empaths in the world, you can serve as a leader. Through your behavior, your knowledge, even on the level of your aura, you can serve as a role model for every empath you meet.

True spiritual lessons are caught, not taught.

Living as a balanced, powerful empath, you're going to help innumerable people through your example.

Becoming The Most Important Person in The Room just might be the start of a new and stronger way of living in the world.

But let's get personal. What will Empath Empowerment mean for *your* life, now and in the future? As we end our 30-Day Plan, here's one last assignment, just for today.

Your Assignment for Day 30

At random times today, dream a bit. Dream about the future you'd like to step into as a high-functioning, skilled empath.

Already you're living in balance, with growing awareness of your gift(s). How might all this skill mature by ten years from now? Here are my predictions.

1. You'll be able to do Skilled Empath Merges at will. Safely.
2. Almost never will you slip into unskilled empath merge.
3. You'll develop discernment about when it is wise to do a Skilled Empath Merge.

4. And you'll also feel comfortable using that skill set very, very sparingly.
5. Everywhere you go, you'll feel like The Most Important Person in The Room.
6. Yet you can freely appreciate how others also are entitled to feel like The Most Important Person in The Room. You'll be able to serve them and learn from them, bringing all due respect.
7. Each day that you live on earth, you'll develop greater appreciation for who you are as a person and also for Otherness.

How open can your heart be? Could you spontaneously stop judging people because you find such magnificence in them? Will your Skilled Empath Merges gradually take on a quality of sacredness?

Dressed in your glorious human identity, living inside your own box, how graceful and glorious can that human life of yours become?

Besides leaving you with these questions, I'd like to offer you this final bit of advice.

Skilled Empath Merging with people, by choice, is always a high. Yet it can be compared to eating ice cream and candy.

Treat yourself. Consider it your reward for attending that tough place I call "Earth School." Maybe even think of it like eating a communion wafer.

But also eat your vegetables, okay?

Continue Your Discoveries as an Empath

At Rose Rosetree's Website You'll Find

Empath Empowerment Book 2:
The Empowered Empath — Quick & Easy
Empath Empowerment Book 3:
The Empowered Empath: Owning, Embracing and Managing Your Special Gifts
Empath Empowerment Book 4:
The Master Empath: Turning on Your Empath Gifts at Will — In Love, Business and Friendship

Other Goodies? Galore!

- Empath Empowerment® Online Workshops and more highly interactive online, on-demand workshops.
- Join the lively informal online community at Rose's blog (44,000 comments and counting), "Deeper Perception Made Practical."
- Sign up for the free monthly e-newsletter, "Reading Life Deeper."
- Personal sessions by phone or webcam. For details, go to www.rose-rosetree.com and click on SESSIONS.
- More books by Rose Rosetree are available to teach you RES Energy READING skills and Energy HEALING skills. There's even Enlightenment Coaching.

WWW.ROSE-ROSETREE.COM

Share Your Experiences, Skilled Empaths

Easy to get and effortless — that's your new flow of information from Skilled Empath Merge. You can do it in person, from streaming images, from photographs. Using techniques learned here, you have so many ways for safe exploring. It's easy, too.

Do you know what can be hard? Getting book reviews.

Here is where you can help other empaths, you Bold Explorer. Please write a review of this book, then share it at Amazon.com, barnesandnoble.com, goodreads.com, and any other book review websites you know. Even a couple of sentences can make such a difference for other empaths.

You'll also be giving back to this indie publisher, who strives to bring innovation to spiritual self-help... and always do it with integrity.

What else? As a skilled empath you may start collecting stories, as I do. Well, yours might be perfect for my future books or at the blog "Deeper Perception Made Practical."

I would love to read your tales of triumph and discovery. Send them to Rose Rosetree, 116 Hillsdale Drive, Sterling, VA 20164. Email to rose@rose-rosetree.com

It's so exciting. You are among the first skilled empaths in the world. It has been such an honor to guide you through this 30-Day Plan for Empath Empowerment.

Bring your special wisdom into this world, bolstered by all your new skills!

www.ingramcontent.com/pod-product-compliance
Lightning Source LLC
Chambersburg PA
CBHW071603080526
44588CB00010B/998